The Single-Handers

The Single-Handers

Graeme Cook

HART-DAVIS, MACGIBBON
GRANADA PUBLISHING
London Toronto Sydney New York

Published by Granada Publishing in
Hart-Davis, MacGibbon Ltd 1977

Granada Publishing Limited
Frogmore, St Albans, Herts AL2 2NF
and
3 Upper James Street, London W1R 4BP
1221 Avenue of the Americas, New York, NY 10020 USA
117 York Street, Sydney, NSW 2000, Australia
100 Skyway Avenue, Toronto, Ontario, Canada M9W 3A6
Trio City, Coventry Street, Johannesburg 2001, South Africa

Copyright © Graeme Cook 1977

ISBN 0 246 10948 3

Filmset in 'Monophoto' Baskerville 11 on 12 pt by
Richard Clay (The Chaucer Press), Ltd, Bungay, Suffolk
and printed in Great Britain by
Fletcher & Son Ltd, Norwich

To
Linda and Roger

Acknowledgements

I should like to express my most sincere gratitude to the authors and publishers who generously gave their permission to draw upon their works for background and technical information. I am indebted also to the staff of Lancaster Public Library, the Ministry of Defence, the Imperial War Museum and especially to Fidelma, who was a constant source of encouragement.

G.C.
Lancaster, 1977

Contents

Introduction

The battle zones of two world wars provided the backdrop for drama of many kinds. On land, men fought in armies large and small; at sea in fleets and flotillas of ships; in the air with flights, squadrons or great waves of aeroplanes. Side by side they engaged in bloody conflict, from time to time immersed in the gore of hellish duels. Together they found the glory of victory or suffered the humiliation of defeat. They risked death, swift or slow and agonising, or worse still horrific mutilation that would scar them for life, mark them as grotesque curios to be gaped at in their wheel-chairs, on crutches, with artificial limbs or bodies re-built by the skill of the plastic surgeon.

For those who fought *en masse*, the spur to heroic deed or the very act of 'going over the top' was frequently the fear of losing face. But more often, heroism was prompted in the heat of battle by compassion for the wounded, screaming man lying yards away amid a hail of enemy fire. What man could leave a comrade there to die? Then there were those who launched themselves into courageous acts stirred by frustration or downright anger, the death of a friend, a moment when reason was cast aside and a mad determination overtook the mind to throw men into deeds of incredible daring against impossible odds. These were the 'spur of the moment' acts.

But what of those who fought *alone* against a foe . . . without a friend? The lone fighter pilot scouring the skies for an enemy of unknown strength with no one to come to his aid, relying upon his skill and wit to win the day, or perish with no ally to rescue him? What of the prisoner of war who breaks out of one prison, only to find himself in the prison of hostile territory with no helping hand to guide him on his way? What too of the spy who haunted the shadows, seeking secret information to relay to his masters from an alien land. His penalty was invariably the gallows or the firing squad if he were caught.

These were the 'loners' and it is about such men that this book is written . . .

1

Gunther Pluschow

George Mine rolled the saliva around in his mouth, parted his lips and ejected the fluid in a jet-like stream. His aim was perfect. The slimy mucus landed with a *splat* in the already filthy gutter of the grimy Tilbury street in London's dockland. He had hardly faltered in his pace and continued shambling along the street, heading for an eating-house on the street corner. It was midday. The lunch parlour was the goal of many others who streamed along the street, most of them workmen. But their pace was quicker than Mine's, hastened by hunger brought on by a hard morning's work in the docks. They strode past him with purpose in their steps while he made way with lethargic slowness. Had anyone bothered to look his way they'd have seen the stamp of a man without a job. His face was glum, his eyes sullen and his brow furrowed but unseen under the peak of a black seaman's cap pulled carelessly down upon his head. The stubble of a few days' growth of beard added the final touch to the façade of a man who had lost his purpose. Mine's jacket and trousers were creased from nights of sleeping rough. The boots that dragged unwillingly along the pavement were coated with dirt and down at the heel. The laces were broken but mended again several times. Mine was a down-and-out and none of the passers-by cared a damn. But nothing could have pleased George Mine more. He was part of the scene; he merged into it as unobtrusively as a chameleon – and that was precisely what he wanted.

At last he reached the doorway of the eating parlour and the sheer weight of humanity fighting its way through the door carried him inside. The smell of dirty, perspiring bodies, stale beer and smoke mixed with the aroma of cooking assaulted his nostrils. He gulped and his stomach heaved. The reaction was not that of a hungry man, not that of a man craving for food. He had tasted the finer things of life in better days but compulsion drove him on. He forged a way through the heavy screen of tobacco smoke towards a long table, where workmen sat, greedily stuffing their mouths with the greasy swill on their plates. Mine paused for a moment, not knowing quite what to do. He had never been in such a place but he soon cottoned on to the form. Those around him grabbed the first available seat and sat waiting for service. There was no menu. One ate what one was given and when Mine had found a seat, a plate was unceremoniously placed before him, together with a pint of dark stout topped with a creamy-white head. He took a good pull at the stout which, to his surprise, had a refreshing tang to it. Then he was about to attack the food on his plate when a gruff, cockney voice only inches from his ear arrested him.

'Eight pence, mate,' the voice said, more in the tone of a demand than a request. Mine searched deep in his pocket and found the required amount which he passed to the waiter without a word. Then he turned his attention once more to the plate before him.

The workman opposite him scooped up the round green peas which floated in gravy and, balancing half a dozen or more on his knife, slid them into his mouth. Mine, anxious to conform, tried to imitate his masterly technique, but failed miserably. The result was a lapful of greasy peas.

It was perhaps his inability to cope with a few simple peas or the fact that he was a stranger that prompted a burly workman to place a hand upon his shoulder. Mine gave a slight jump. Suddenly he was nervous.

'Hey, where's your papers?' the intruder demanded. For a moment Mine was visibly flustered.

'Papers?' he began, stalling for time. 'I – eh – I have forgotten them. I don't have them with me . . .' By now there was a hint of panic in his voice and in his eyes. He looked towards the door. He felt like making a bolt for it. He had no papers. The man who towered over Mine looked suspiciously at him. There was the slightest hint of a foreign accent in Mine's voice.

'Well, we'll have to see about this, won't we? Can't come in 'ere without papers. You just hang about, mate, and I'll find out just what we're goin' to do with you.'

At that he left. Mine saw him go towards a telephone. But there was no time for him to do anything about it. The barman had overheard the conversation and joined in.

'Forgotten your papers have you?' he asked.

'Yes. I – ' Mine fumbled for an excuse. 'I left them on my ship.'

The barman detected the foreign accent.

'You ain't British are you? Where d'you hail from an' wot's yer name?'

'George Mine,' he admitted. 'That's my name – George Mine. I'm a seaman; a naturalised American. I'm off the old four-masted barque *Ohio*. She is lying upriver. I just came ashore for a few hours and came in here for something to eat. I left my papers behind on the ship.'

'Well, that explains it, then,' the barman thought aloud. 'See, it's like this. This is a private club. You've gotta be a member before you can eat here. It's for the workers only, see?'

Mine tried his best not to show his relief. It was his membership papers that had been requested, not identity papers as he had feared.

'Look, mate,' the barman said. 'If you want to join the club you can – then you can come in 'ere as often as you like. It'll cost you three bob. How about it?'

'Yes, yes, certainly. I'd like to join. Here, three shillings.'

'Right, mate,' the barman said in a satisfied tone, 'you're now a member of the Tilbury Social Democratic Trades Union. You can eat 'ere as often as you want an' you're welcome. Now we've gotta fix yer up with a badge, like the rest of us.'

The barman disappeared for a short while, then returned and threaded a thin red ribbon through the top buttonhole in Mine's jacket. George Mine was now a fully paid-up member of the union. What the barman failed to appreciate was that he had just performed a unique ceremony. He had opened the portals of his 'exclusive' club to the most wanted man in Britain . . .

The First World War was still in its infancy when George Mine enrolled in the workers' union but the green fields of northern Europe had already been transformed into gory swamps, stained by the blood of soldiers locked in mortal conflict. Lord Kitchener's cry to the youth of Britain 'Your Country Needs

You' echoed throughout the land and thousands of young men answered the call to become cannon-fodder for the German guns. At sea too, the German Kaiser's U-boats and surface raiders were attempting to strangle Britain into defeat by severing her tenuous sea-link with North America along which her supplies flowed. In the North Sea they foraged for prey among the British merchantmen that plied these waters. It was in the East End dockland of London that many of these cargo ships unloaded their life-saving cargoes.

Ordinary Seaman George Mine was unwittingly accepted by that barman as being one of the brave sailors who ran the gauntlet of the German sea war. True, he was a naval man, but he was no ordinary seaman, no naturalised American, no down-and-out, luckless tramp scrounging a meal – nor indeed was he George Mine. Had the barman paid greater heed to the banner headlines in the daily newspapers or the talk of the workers who frequented his eating parlour; had he noticed the strong guttural accent in Mine's English speech, *he* might have become the focus of the newspaper headlines as the man who caught the hunted fugitive Lieutenant Gunther Pluschow of the Kaiser's Navy and more recently an inmate of Donington Hall, a prisoner of war camp for officers near Derby.

The gravity of Pluschow's plight was considerable ... a German escaper on the run from a whole nation. But then Pluschow was no newcomer to being hunted. Already he had become accomplished in the art of evasion, so expert indeed that he had played the fox in the hunt halfway around the world ...

Lieutenant Gunther Pluschow found himself in the thick of the fighting when Japan and Germany plunged into war in 1914. He was at the time serving as a pilot in the Kaiser's navy and based at Tsing-Tao, the capital of the Chinese German Protectorate. He was the senior officer in charge of two single-seater spotter planes which used the racecourse in the city as an airfield.

Pluschow's aeroplanes were flimsy biplanes, mere embryonic models of the fighters which would do battle over the trenches of northern France at the height of the air war in Europe. They were fashioned out of wood with stretched canvas covering the airframe. Light and unwieldy they were easy game for the eccentricities of the weather. A strong wind made flying in one of these aircraft a herculean struggle against the elements. It must be remembered that the first successful powered flight in a fixed wing aircraft had taken place only eleven years earlier and flying was still very much in its infancy. The performance of a simple loop in one of these craft was a feat of considerable daring. There were no parachutes on board with which to escape from a stricken aircraft. If something were to go wrong in the air the result was all too often a grisly death. Flying in 1914 demanded a spirit of adventure and a disregard for danger. Pluschow had both of these and more.

When Germany and Japan went to war, bitter and bloody fighting ensued upon the ground. Teeming hordes of Japanese overran vast areas of China, leaving massacre and slaughter in their wake. Warfare had not, as yet, become a mechanised affair. The man and his weapon combined with artillery and the strategy of past wars won the day. The day of the cavalry charge was not past. The machine had yet to dominate the battlefield. And the handful of aircraft which were available to the armed forces had not become fighting weapons. The generals had not yet grasped the potential of the aeroplane as a fighting machine, but after much persuasion they had accepted it as a useful tool for observing the enemy's positions. With the aeroplane's ability to fly high, the pilot got an uninterrupted view of the landscape for miles around. What an advantage it would be, the generals thought, if they could precisely locate the positions of enemy artillery and troops and then bring their own guns to bear on them. Thus, the aeroplane was given the role of artillery spotter and it was to this somewhat passive pursuit that Pluschow and his two single-seaters were detailed. Day after day, he flew high above the Japanese lines and, with the use of field glasses, got a clear view of their gun positions. After he had marked them on a map he would 'dash' back to his headquarters and report their positions. It was tame work for a professional fighter. He flew so high in his aircraft that he was immune from the enemy's gunfire, if not from the hazards of the weather. There were no anti-aircraft guns and the Japanese, who were notoriously inaccurate with rifles, took pot-shots at the aircraft but failed to inflict any damage.

The advance of the Japanese army against an inferior Chinese and German army could not be checked. Inexorably, they forged forward, sweeping aside all resistance that lay in their path. The Japanese closed on Tsing-Tao and a barrage of heavy gunfire began. Shells rained down upon the city, buildings collapsed, limbs were torn from their torsos. The racecourse, with its two small aircraft received a direct hit. It exploded in a great ball of flame, disintegrating and showering the expanse of green with flaming fragments. Shrapnel from the explosion perforated the other aircraft, leaving ragged gashes in her canvas, but she was otherwise unharmed. Pluschow was ordered to fly out of Tsing-Tao in the only remaining aeroplane. It was clear the city could not withstand the onslaught much longer. It was bound to succumb to the might of the Imperial Japanese Army. Pluschow determined to flee the city to fight again.

Still the bombardment continued. Shells blasted great craters out of the racecourse while Pluschow clambered into the cramped cockpit of the aircraft. A mechanic swung the aeroplane's propeller and the engine burst into life. Pluschow eagerly scanned the pock-marked field for a clear strip of grass from which to take off. The shells fell closer, casting tons of earth skyward and showering the pilot as he manoeuvred the plane between the holes in the earth. The aircraft rocked crazily as a shell thudded into the ground nearby and exploded. The shock wave from the blast caught the wing and lifted Pluschow's aeroplane half into the air. She spun in a crazy gyration then settled with a bump. Thick black smoke swept across the field, blinding Pluschow and stinging his eyes. He choked as it found its way into his mouth and nose but he pressed on.

At last he broke through the screen of smoke and before him lay a reasonably level stretch of grass. Pluschow opened up the throttle and the plane careered forward, the sound of the engine drowned by the din of the bombardment. The plane gathered speed until at last Pluschow pulled gently back on the control column. For a few moments it hugged the ground, unwilling to lift into the air, preferring to take cover on the ground. Then, Pluschow felt her free herself from the grass and rock as she was caught in the confusion of air currents wrought by the exploding shells. At full throttle, the aircraft clawed its way higher into the sky, skimming over the perimeter of the racecourse, over the panorama of destruction that lay below. Even here Pluschow was not safe. The whine of transient shells deafened the pilot as they curved across the sky, narrowly missing the aeroplane.

As the plane gained more height, Pluschow allowed himself a moment's glance downward at the city. It was a scene of confusion. Fires raged and parts of the city were masked by smoke.

He could see streams of minute figures running for their lives from the cataclysm. Rivers of humanity streaming through the narrow streets. If there was a hell, it was surely down there, Pluschow thought, and he cursed the Japanese and their Emperor.

Finally the city slipped away beneath him as he set course for neutral China. Below him were the hills and paddy-fields, peaceful and undisturbed by the fury of the war that raged not far off. Soon these fields would run red with the blood of the opposing sides. Now Pluschow felt curiously detached from the war. The slipstream flowed into the cockpit bringing with it the sweet smell of fresh air, tinged only by the hint of burning fuel. But it cleansed his smoke-choked tubes and he felt refreshed as the aeroplane droned over the quiet countryside below. Here, high above the troubled land of China, he felt at peace and he had to jolt himself back to reality. Unable to refuel his aircraft before taking off, she was now low on petrol. A quick mental calculation told him the worst. He would be lucky indeed if he made it into neutral China for that was the only place he could hope to seek succour from the Japanese. He knew his rightful place was in Europe, fighting for the Fatherland, not here thousands of miles away in this hot, sweltering climate. If the war were to be won, then it would be in Europe and he determined that he would be in the thick of it. How he would get there he did not know but he was resolute in his determination to try – or die in the attempt.

As the aircraft progressed slowly over the hills and plateaux that abounded in that region, Pluschow's eyes kept a careful watch on the fuel gauge as it gradually fell. Would she hold out? Would he make it?

Ahead lay Hai-dschow but as he saw the city on the shimmering horizon the engine spluttered and coughed. The plane jolted, then the engine rasped into life once more but only for a moment. The tanks were dry. Suddenly there was silence, broken only by the swish of the air over the tattered airframe. Pluschow scanned the countryside beneath him, searching for a suitable landing-place, while he used all his skill to maintain height by gliding. The terrain below was hilly and each hillside was broken up in steps to form rice fields. The watery terraces were everywhere, with the thin rice grass protruding from their flooded surfaces. There was nowhere safe to land, no flat stretches of land; just rice fields everywhere.

Pluschow circled about the sky losing height and settling towards a cleft in the land. As he gradually neared the expanse of water, the ground seemed to dash towards him in a blurred rush. He levelled off and prepared to land, keeping the nose of the aircraft as high as he could without obstructing his view. The sun, burning down from above, reflected off the water and glared bright silver, half-blinding him. Now he was only feet from the water. Pluschow hauled back on the control column. The nose reared upwards and the aircraft stalled. The tail hit the water and he was thrown forward as the water bit and arrested the aircraft in its path. Like a whiplash the nose fell into the water, amid an almighty splash. The aircraft, driven on by the impetus of its forward movement, thrust through the rice grass tearing it out of the ground. Then the grass wrapped itself around the fixed undercarriage, clogged the engine ports and gripped the lower wings.

The impact stunned Pluschow. His head bounced off the rubber padding above the control column and rebounded. Then the aircraft stopped. There was utter silence, an eery quiet in which Pluschow, dazed and bruised by the crash, struggled to regain his senses. In the moments after the crash, he could make no sense of the situation. Why were his feet in water? There was no pain; just a numbness. No sound – nothing. He quizzed himself. Was he dead? Why couldn't he move his body? He couldn't understand it. Then, through the mist of concussion, realisation dawned. He was trapped in the cramped cockpit by broken wood and twisted metal while water seeped into the lower part of the cockpit. He tried to move his hands and a jarring pain shot up his arm and tortured his head. He forced his hands to the lap belt which he undid slowly. He raised his head to look around. His vision was blurred. He felt drunk, but he narrowed his eyes straining to make sense out of the blur of the countryside around him. Gradually, like the adjustment of a camera lens, the blur came into focus. The scene brought the truth flooding back to him. Pluschow hauled himself up in the cockpit and half jumped, half fell headlong into the shallow water of the rice field. The water brought him quickly to his senses. The aircraft was a wreck. He could see that clearly enough. Bits of it were strewn around the paddy field. He marvelled that he had got out alive, but now he was faced with getting help and making his way around the world to the Fatherland.

Standing knee-deep in the water, Pluschow took stock of the situation. He was battered and bruised but, apart from that, miraculously unscathed. He waded over to the aircraft, took what small possessions he could find and stuffed them into his pockets. Then, still light-headed, he staggered away from the wreck.

As he regained his strength, the shock of the event that had just occurred engulfed him. He was thousands of miles away from Germany; between him and home lay the continent of Asia if he chose the overland route or two great oceans and a continent if he chose to go by sea. One thing was certain; no matter which route he chose, he would need help. He had little money, certainly not enough to get him more than halfway round the world but he resolved that somehow he would make it back to the Fatherland.

The fingers of Imperial Germany stretched far across the world and he knew that he would find his fellow countrymen somewhere in the bigger cities of neutral China if he searched closely enough. Refreshed by this thought, Pluschow got to his feet and began to walk in the direction of Hai-dschow.

Pluschow had to take frequent rests on that trek before finally he reached the perimeter of the city, which lay on a river. His knowledge of the geography of that part of China was sketchy but he did know that the river found its way to the sea, west of the port of Nanking, where he hoped to find a ship which would take him across the Pacific Ocean to the United States, which was still neutral, and then on to Germany.

The easiest and probably the only way from Hai-dschow to Nanking was by river, and after much haggling Pluschow secured a place on one of the junks. He boarded her immediately and she sailed on the tide.

After what seemed like an eternity, the junk put in to Nanking. Pluschow bade his shipmates goodbye and stepped ashore, right into the hands of the Chinese port authorities. He was immediately subjected to lengthy questioning during which he held back nothing. What reason was there to do so, he thought. China was neutral and had nothing to do with the war. But that was where Pluschow had made his first mistake. The Chinese informed him that he would be detained in an internment camp for the duration of the war. Pluschow was thunderstruck, and it was a dejected and dispirited man who was led away to gaol by his Chinese guards. But as he was marched between his guards along the streets towards the gaol he resolved to make a bolt for it.

He chose his moment carefully. He watched his guards. They appeared singularly uninterested in the whole affair. An alley-way lay ahead. This was it. When they were abreast of it, Pluschow vanished, leaving behind a bewildered pair of Chinese. The streets were crowded and soon he was lost in the throng of people, putting as much distance between himself and his former guards as he could without attracting attention by running.

Pluschow pushed on through the crowds, careless of the direction in which he was going, content only to know that the guards had lost him. Furtive glances behind him proved that he was not being followed but he knew that he would have to get out of Nanking quickly before a full-scale search could be mounted. The quickest way out of the city was by rail and after some searching Pluschow found the railway station where he boarded a train for Shanghai. There, he would be less obtrusive in an international port which thronged with sailors of all nation-alities.

Forewarned by his experience in Nanking, he took every precaution to make himself as inconspicuous as he could when he alighted from the train in busy Shanghai. He slipped out of the railway station unnoticed. No one gave him as much as a sideways glance. Pluschow was elated at his success but his high spirits had to be tempered with caution. Every step he took could be into the hands of the Chinese. He wanted above all else to make contact with some of his fellow countrymen and by making some prudent enquiries, he succeeded in doing just that.

Like the peoples of most nationalities in a foreign country the Germans in Shanghai formed themselves into a tight commun-ity. They were civilians and non-combatants who were therefore not subject to internment and were at liberty to move freely about the city. When Pluschow made his plight known to them, they were eager to help: he was absorbed into the community and 'lost'. Hiding up in a German household, his new-found friends set to work preparing to get him out of the country.

There were two vital prerequisites to his escape from China. First, and most obviously, not to get caught by the Chinese; and secondly to assume a new identity. The former was not too difficult since there were many Germans willing to give him succour in their homes. The second, however, posed a more serious problem. But he was assured by his friends that it was not an insurmountable one. He would have to obtain forged identity papers. As the days passed while this was put in hand, Pluschow found himself becoming impatient. But things like manufacturing a forged passport took time and Pluschow simply had to wait.

It was clear that he could not travel as a German since this might invite questions. His friends chose to make him British and a passport was procured for him in the name of MacGarvin. His cover story was that he was the representative of the Singer Sewing Machine Company and was returning to Britain via the United States after a tour in China. It was a plausible, if dangerous, disguise. Pluschow had a strong German accent which was instantly noticeable in spite of his near perfect English vocabulary.

He was found a cabin aboard an American ship, the SS *Mongolia*, which was bound for North America. The choice of the *Mongolia* was a good one, for the doctor on board was also a 'friend'.

When the *Mongolia* put into the Japanese harbour of Nagasaki, the Japanese port police who boarded to inspect her and check the passenger list found that one of the passengers had been taken ill and was confined to his cabin. The doctor advised the police not to enter the cabin as the disease was highly infectious. They did not argue with him and Pluschow remained 'desperately ill' behind his cabin door, out of sight of the Japanese. When the *Mongolia* reached Kobe, Pluschow was still very 'ill', too ill to be disturbed. In fact his illness continued until after the ship had left Yokohama when Pluschow made a remarkable recovery. Thanks to the doctor, Pluschow had overcome another hurdle. The remainder of the voyage passed without event and the *Mongolia* docked at San Francisco, where Pluschow had to face the American customs officials. 'Mr MacGarvin' passed through customs without any trouble and, using money supplied to him by his German friends in Shanghai, crossed the United States to New York.

Like Shanghai but on a much bigger scale, there were Germans here eager to help a runaway on his way. So, after making contact with them, Gunther Pluschow now became Ernst Suse, Swiss locksmith, en route to his native land and due to sail on the Italian steamer *Duca degli Abruzzi*. The ship sailed out of New York and into the Atlantic with Pluschow on board. He was astonished at the number of other Swiss nationals on board the ship – all of them travelling to Naples and then Switzerland. It soon became clear that there was a veritable flood of Germans, posing as Swiss, steaming across the Atlantic to join forces with their brothers at arms who were fighting in Europe.

Pluschow might have sailed into Naples unmolested and reached the Fatherland had it not been for an unfortunate occurrence: the *Duca degli Abruzzi* made an unscheduled stop at the British colony of Gibraltar. No sooner had she tied up than the ship was boarded by a British naval patrol. The officer in charge of the patrol noticed on examining the passports of the passengers the uncommon number of 'Swiss' subjects and this gave rise to suspicion. It did not take much questioning to establish that some of them at least were Germans. All of them were arrested, including Pluschow, and taken into custody where they were subjected to searching and highly professional interrogation. Pluschow's cover was 'blown' and he found himself heading north under armed guard. He was bound for England and incarceration as a prisoner of war. So tight was the security surrounding him during that journey that he had no hope of escape. The British now knew who he was and they were determined that he would stay in their clutches for as long as the war lasted. Pluschow, on the other hand, was equally determined that he would not.

But Pluschow's determination took something of a knock when he saw the 'camp' to which he was sent. It was Donington Hall, a seventeenth century manor house set in enormous grounds near Derby which had been commandeered by the army for use as an officers' prisoner of war camp when the first prisoners were captured after the outbreak of war. The huge house was surrounded by dense entanglements of barbed wire. Inside, the accommodation was good. The British apparently intended making their 'guests' as comfortable as possible, but at the same time making absolutely sure that they remained where they were. Escape was impossible, Pluschow was informed upon his arrival, and glancing around the fencing and the system of guards he began to believe that to be true.

Pluschow, unlike some of his brother officers, never did settle easily into imprisonment, but he threw himself with considerable fervour into the activities of camp life, notably hockey which he played with great skill. He reasoned, quite rightly, that if he were to make a bid for freedom, he would have to be fit and his daily game of hockey kept him in trim.

Apart from his inherent sense of duty to the Kaiser there was one other factor which goaded him into making his escape – sheer boredom. He was twenty-nine at the time and an active man, unused to being penned in. He hated it, every moment of it. Imprisonment ate away at him like a cancer and his resolution to break out was only heightened when he received letters from home.

Every day, he would walk the fence. It loomed large and forbidding but he saw it as a challenge. If only he could get to the other side, he was sure he could make it. After all he had come most of the way round the world and he was not going to let a few strands of barbed wire or the English Channel stand in his way.

Working on the precept that two heads were better than one, Pluschow recruited a fellow naval officer, equally determined in his resolve to escape, with whom he could make a break. They became constant companions, spending much of their waking hours investigating the possibility of a break out. They searched for a flaw in the British defences, timing sentries on their 'beats', looking for 'blind spots' in the sentry cover of the wire – and they found one, a point in the wire which, at a given time, could not be seen by the sentries and over which they could climb.

POW camps then were far from being the sophisticated prisons of the Second World War. There were no electrified fences, no tall machine-gun towers, no mine-fields ringing the camp – but there were frequent roll-calls and this was to be one of his problems in escaping from the Hall. He and his companion would have to make their break after dark and there was a roll-call before the prisoners retired to bed. Some means had to be devised whereby the roll-call was correct and yet neither Pluschow nor his fellow escaper was present. It was a tricky puzzle but they found a solution. They resorted to an old escaper's trick by feigning illness while the roll-call was taking place. They were reported as being ill and after the roll-call, two confidants took their place in their respective beds. In the meantime, Pluschow and his companion were already in hiding in the grounds of the Hall. All they had to do then was wait for the right moment. It was a tense time for them. They lay within earshot of the sentries. They could hear them pacing their beats, stopping at intervals to have a chat with their comrades. Everything was peaceful. The lights in the dormitories blinked and went out, plunging the Hall into darkness.

The wearing of civilian clothes in the camp was not forbidden, since many of the inmates had lost their uniforms before or during capture and were supplied with an assortment of clothing. It was therefore not difficult for both Pluschow and his companion to fit themselves out with passable suits of clothes. Both had chosen typical seamen's outfits, since it was their intention to head for London in the hope that they might stow away on a ship which would take them to Europe, preferably Holland, which was neutral and bordered on Germany. Getting out of Donington Hall was one thing – getting across the 'ditch' that separated them from friendly territory was quite another. It was their greatest barrier.

Both men peered anxiously towards the barbed wire entanglement. It was dark and in the half light they could detect no hint of the presence of a sentry near 'their' bit of fence. It was now or never. Bending low to diminish their size they shot across the open ground between them and the wire. No yell of alarm came; nor the report and whine of a shot. So far so good. Their hearts thumped and were almost audible to them as they threaded their way through the wire and scrambled over it. Both had to fight the urge to curse as their clothes were snared on the protruding barbs but at last they were over. Still they moved with care. An eagle-eyed sentry could still sight them and their efforts would have been to no avail. But all remained peaceful. With growing optimism, they crept farther away from the fence. Still no cry of alarm. The farther they got, the more confident they became. On they went, hardly daring to admit to each other that they had in fact made it.

Their first target, Derby, was some thirty miles from the Hall and, if they were to evade detection when 'the balloon went up' and the troops were sent out after them, they had to cover that distance in one night. Both men walked at a fierce pace, which rarely slackened that night until they reached Derby and headed for the railway station.

Pluschow and his fellow escaper were already well on their way to London when all hell was let loose at Donington Hall. As soon as their escape was discovered a nation-wide alert went out, but by then the birds had flown quite a distance. They alighted from the train and wisely decided to part company and fend for themselves. After all, they reasoned, the British troops, police and indeed civilians would be on the look-out for two escapers and their chances of escape would be greater if each was on his own.

Pluschow's companion did not last long as a free man. He was recaptured and returned to imprisonment. Pluschow, on the other hand, had so far escaped detection. But he was a tense man. Already the newspapers bore headlines warning of the escape. They contained a description of Pluschow – and a damning tip as to how he could be recognised. One newspaper report read:

MUCH ESCAPED FUGITIVE

By the Chinese dragon clue the authorities still hope to trace Lieutenant Gunther Pluschow, of the German Navy, who escaped from Donington Hall on Monday. The dragon is tattooed on the fugitive's left arm in Oriental colours. It was probably worked by a native artist, for although but twenty-nine years of age, Pluschow has had an adventurous career in the Kaiser's Navy.

He was in Tsing-Tao when the British and Japanese besieged that German fortress. Shortly before it fell, Pluschow escaped in an aeroplane, and some weeks later he was found on board a trading vessel at Gibraltar.

He will probably endeavour to sign on as a seaman in a neutral ship sailing from a British port, and, with this in view, a very careful watch is being kept on all the ports throughout the country. Pluschow is a typical sailor, about 5 feet 6 inches in height, with fair hair and fresh complexion. He would pass for a Dutchman with his broken English. Nothing he can do can remove the Chinese dragon from his left arm, and his recapture should be but a matter of time.

Pluschow cursed the day he had had his arm tattooed but he realised that that would only come to light if he were challenged. He therefore took great care to avoid taking off his jacket. As to his fair hair, the ingenious Pluschow had already taken care of that. By the use of some vaseline and black boot polish, he had become dark haired. As to his fresh complexion, that very soon disappeared after a few nights roughing it around London. Lack of sleep brought the gaunt features of a hungry man to his face.

The escaper, who had been financed from 'funds' secretly acquired at Donington Hall, scrounged around London's dockland in search of a Dutch steamer which would take him to Holland and freedom, but without success. Every day he spent at large in England heightened the chances of his discovery and since he had no papers, not even forged ones, there would be no talking his way out of a fix.

Luck plays a large part in the fortunes of the escaper and it visited the dispirited Pluschow when he was travelling on the top deck of a bus. Sitting behind two men, he found himself listening to their conversation. Both men were clearly in the shipping business and they talked of imminent sailings from London. Pluschow had to restrain himself from leaning forward to hear more clearly when the word Holland came into the conversation. Pluschow's interpretation of the facts were sketchy, largely owing to the noise of the bus, but he gleaned from the conversation that every morning at seven o'clock, a Dutch steamer left Tilbury docks for Flushing. That was all he wanted to hear and left the bus at the next stop.

Over-excited at the news, Pluschow sensibly decided to take a rest first and consider his next move before making for Tilbury. He chose the quiet solitude of a church in which to work out his plan of action. He had been a frequent visitor to London's churches over the past few days, not to seek the help of God in his quest for freedom, but to catch up on his sleep under the guise of being deep in prayer.

After a short mental debate, Pluschow left the church and made his way to Blackfriars station where he boarded a train bound for Tilbury. Within the hour, he was off the train and making his way towards the docks. But after he had walked the length of the docks twice, it was clear that his Dutch ship was not there. Now he felt glum and downhearted. He left the docks and shuffled along the streets which bordered them, trying to convince himself that the conversation he had overheard on the bus was not some cruel dream and a figment of his tired imagination. Little wonder then that, when he approached the corner eating parlour, he bore the mark of a dejected man. Small wonder too that, when the workman asked for his papers, he was shocked and nervous for that could have been the end of his freedom in London . . .

As he scooped the last of the peas from his plate, Pluschow was relieved at the outcome of his close shave but puzzled as to what he should do next. He drained the dregs from his glass of stout and left his 'club'. One thing was certain – he dared not leave the river and he resolved to keep a day and night watch on the ships that came into Tilbury. For this he had to find a suitable vantage-point.

Assuming the outward appearance of a down-and-out once more, Pluschow made his way to the riverside where he found a patch of grass. From here he had a clear view of the Thames. It was ideal and he lay down, as if taking a nap but in fact keeping a watchful eye on the river traffic.

He lay there for three hours, carefully examining every vessel that passed but none of them was Dutch. He was beginning to give up hope when, at about four o'clock, a steamer hove into sight. She was a proud-looking ship and fast with it but at a distance there was little to say what her nationality was. As she drew nearer, he saw the Dutch flag flying at the ship's stern. Surely this must be her, he thought. The ship slowed and dropped anchor. Emblazoned upon her bow was her name *Mecklenburg*. Pluschow was stunned. The coincidence was startling. He had been born and bred in Mecklenburg-Schwerin. Surely this was a good omen. Would this be the ship that would bear him across the English Channel to freedom?

He watched her as she tied up to a buoy closer to the opposite shore of the river. He had to get nearer to her so that he could plan just how to get on board this 'glorious vessel'. Nearby was the point from which the ferry-boat transported passengers over to Gravesend and Pluschow made for it.

By the time the ferry docked, the tramp had made something of a transformation. His shambling gait was gone. The dull, sullen face became alive, the blue eyes bright and alert in expectation, the sailor's cap which had been pulled down to obscure his solemn face now took on a rakish, jaunty angle. He stepped off the gangway and on to the shore. This change in mood gave him a fresh identity. He now looked for all the world like a sailor, albeit a pretty scruffy specimen, but a tar for all that. And this was precisely the new image he wanted to present. Whistling a nautical note or two he made his way along the shore-line, walking with a typical seaman's roll until he reached a point almost opposite the *Mecklenburg*. To get a good view of her, he had to scramble over towering rubbish tips and into what appeared to be a wood-yard where pile upon pile of cut wood was stacked to season. Here he found himself a nook, made more acceptable by the presence of a few bales of hay which formed a comfortable bed, upon which to rest until the time was right to make for the ship.

Pluschow carried out a thorough survey of the immediate stretch of river. There were two barges moored a little way offshore, not far from his hide. Behind them out in the river lay the *Mecklenburg*. He would wait till nightfall then swim out to the ship, scale the hawser that linked the ship to the buoy and scramble on deck where he would hide away until she reached Holland. With his plan of action firmly decided, Pluschow fell asleep. He awoke a little before midnight. The night was dark, which, although it afforded him protection from prying eyes, made finding his way to the shore difficult. Gingerly he crept towards it. But as he did so the heavens opened and a torrent of rain poured down on him, bringing visibility to only a few yards.

Finally, after slipping and cursing several times, he reached the shore. His intention was to make for the barges, scramble over them then swim the remainder of the distance out to the ship. But when he took a step into what he thought was the sea, there was a pronounced squelch. Mud! Thick, slimy, oozing mud – and it lay between him and the barges. Struggling, he managed a few more laboured steps. Now he could see that the barges were lying high and dry. The tide was out and, but for a small rowing-boat tied up to the stern of one of the barges which barely floated in shallow water, the barges were stuck solid in the mud. Dragging his mud-caked feet, he made his way back through the rain to his hide and lay down on the hay.

He lay awake all night, unable to sleep because of the disappointment he had suffered. Dawn came and with the light he was able to see that his entire body was filthy with a hard coating of mud. Worse, at seven o'clock precisely, the *Mecklenburg* weighed anchor and steamed down river out to the open sea and on to Flushing.

The escaper scraped the mud from his clothes and boots,

doing what he could to smarten up his appearance but it all seemed to no avail. For the rest of the day, he wandered around the docks, hoping that he might discover another neutral ship that he might be able to board surreptitiously. That evening he strode, almost automatically, back to Gravesend and casually glanced towards the river. Then his heart gave a jump. Lying resplendent at her moorings was the Dutch steamer *Princess Juliana*. He couldn't believe his luck. But this time he was to make sure he would not fall into the same trap as he had done the night before. The mud was a menace to which he had no intentions of succumbing.

Pluschow studied the riverside with great care, searching for a suitable launching-point from which he would swim out to the steamer. At last he found what he took to be the ideal place, a stony stretch of shore-line and lying a short way off it, were several rowing-boats, moored to small buoys. If only he could reach one of these he could row the distance out to the ship. Buoyant now at the prospect of what the night might bring, he hid until midnight when he made his way to the stony beach. There, he stripped off his jacket and his boots, which he wrapped up and hid beneath a stone. His other possessions, few as they were, he stuffed in his cap and pulled it firmly down upon his head.

Pluschow waded out into the murky water of the Thames and began to swim. As he did so, the water seeped into his clothing, adding to his weight. Every stroke he took became more difficult, demanding a powerful exertion of his arms. Soon, he was so weighted down that he could go no farther and no amount of will power could thrust him nearer to the small rowing-boat that lay not far away. A fast current caught him, pulling him away from the boat. The water flowed over his head. Shattered with exhaustion, he tried desperately to fight against it. He gulped in mouthfuls of the filthy water, choking himself. He was drowning and, with no strength left in his limbs, it seemed that the river would claim him. A calm came over him as the water found its way into his lungs. Numbed, the manifest sensations of a drowning man overtook him and he lapsed into unconsciousness. Pluschow might have died, had it not been for the current which drove him to the shore. Half in and half out of the water, he lay on the pebbled shore. How long he lay there, he never knew but finally consciousness returned to him. He coughed, and the polluted water spewed up from his stomach and lungs. The sea had delivered him up but he lay shivering with cold, unable to control his trembling limbs

Half crawling and stumbling, he moved from the water's edge, his clothes dripping wet and heavy. As the cloud of semi-consciousness faded from his brain, he was able to think more clearly and, after an hour of rummaging about the shore, he uncovered his boots and jacket. With quaking hands, he tried to wring the water out of his jersey, trousers and socks. His boots and jacket afforded little extra warmth and even when he found his original hide in the wood-piles and wrapped the hay around himself, it did nothing to bring warmth back to him.

In a desperate bid to restore some heat to his body, he threw himself into a frenzy of running and jumping, as much as he could manage considering his weakened state. It helped a little but not enough.

After an eternity of waiting, the sky lightened and blossomed into dawn, a rainy, torrential dawn with an overcast sky which seemed to bode ill for Pluschow. Twice, his attempt to board a Dutch ship had been thwarted. Glumly, he emerged from his hiding-place, more dejected than ever. His sole aim now was to find somwhere warm. He gravitated towards his former haunts, the churches, and there, hugging the radiators, life slowly returned to his body. He left the church and walked, bringing more heat to his body through physical exertion. A meal helped to restore his strength and soon briskness returned to his step.

Pluschow walked the streets of London unnoticed, and wandered into a public square. The sun shone brightly now but still his clothes were wet. He looked bedraggled and beaten. In the middle of the square there was an assembly of people. Unconsciously he wandered towards the throng. It was to be a mistake that almost cost him his freedom. Amid the mass stood a speaker on a platform urging the youth of the nation, and in particular those assembled around the platform, to enlist in the Army and join the fight to defeat the Hun. Without thinking, Pluschow shouldered his way into the crowd, fascinated by the man's oratory. He grinned inwardly at the speaker's exhortations to the crowd. Had they known that one of the foe was in their midst the crowd's reaction might have been instant and violent. But Pluschow's mental mirth was cut short when he was confronted by a veritable giant of a man, resplendent in the uniform of an

Army sergeant. He towered over Pluschow and, with a smile which held more menace than friendliness, began . . .

'An' wot about you, me lad, eh? How d'you fancy yerself in the uniform of the King?'

The sergeant embraced Pluschow's muscular arm in a vice-like grip. Pluschow was too stunned to react.

'Fine strong arms y've got there, son. Now what d'you say. How about getting over there an' givin' the Hun a taste o' British medicine. Eh? Come along, lad. Wot about it?'

Pluschow forced a few words.

'Sorry, Sergeant. I can't do it. I'm an American citizen. I'm a sailor and my captain would not be pleased if I deserted ship to join your Army.'

It was a hastily contrived excuse and a reasonable one, but the sergeant was not to be swayed. He produced a montage of photographs of British soldiers in uniforms of various regiments, as if to tempt the 'American'. This British soldier was tenacious and Pluschow could feel himself getting into deep water. More words might reveal his nationality and to rid himself of the soldier he promised to discuss the matter with his captain and return the following day. Mercifully for the German, the sergeant accepted the promise and moved on to persuade others to answer the call to arms. With that, Pluschow beat a hasty retreat.

He found refuge in the British Museum and from there moved on to spend almost the last remaining money he had on a visit to a music-hall. The brief interlude in the music-hall restored his spirits, although he was conscious of the sideways glances of those who were near him. He stank and there was no hiding it. He had not bathed in days, at least not in a bath. The Thames, notorious in those days for its pollution, clung to him and his clothing, emitting a noxious aroma. He was used to it by now but those he passed by were not and the strong smell made them wince in disgust at the filthy tramp.

He walked back to Gravesend and lay in a small park by the river, going over in his mind his previous attempts at escape and planning his next.

He had failed before because of the capricious tidal flow and the dangerous mud. It was clear that he would only be able to reach the Dutch steamer if he could 'borrow' a rowing-boat tied up at the shore and row the distance out to the Dutch ship. With this in mind, he scouted the shore-line looking for a dinghy. After some searching he found one, but it was tied up at a jetty where a sentry was on guard. But Pluschow was undaunted. That night he would have that dinghy, no matter what the risks involved. He waited until midnight before making a move, then he crept furtively along the fringe of the river towards the wharf. Some inner sense told him that the sentry – or at least his relief – had not deserted his post. Hardly daring to disturb a pebble, he felt his way along the shore. He had taken the precaution of removing his boots, tying the laces together and then slinging them around his neck. Between his teeth he held a knife which he would use without hesitation if the sentry proved bothersome. The night was calm and quiet, disturbed only by muffled, occasional sounds from the docks across the water and the lapping of the Thames upon the stony foreshore. One other sound disturbed the night, the steady tramp of the sentry as he paced his beat.

Pluschow inched forward. He was so close to the sentinel, who stood guard over the jetty that a yawn of tiredness and boredom was clearly audible. A low wall barred his way and with quiet caution, he rolled over it. The small boat was within reach now. In the darkness he felt for the gunwale and scrambled into the boat. To his annoyance it was half full of water and the sudden cold on his feet shocked him. Still the sentry strode up and down the pier and on to the wharf nearby. No time to waste. Pluschow found the oars but to his fury they were locked by chains. Cursing his luck he gingerly felt the chains. By good fortune they were not padlocked and they slid easily away from the oars.

Carefully, Pluschow placed the oars in the rowlocks then with his knife slashed through the rope that held the boat fast to the pier. She was free. He sat amidships and grabbed the oars, gently dipping them into the water and giving strong pulls. The water swilled about his feet but the boat moved away from the shore. His confidence grew as he gained ground and he put more force into his strokes. But as he did so he became aware that with every stroke, more water seeped into the boat. The trickle of water grew to an inrush until it had reached the thwarts. Suddenly the dinghy ground to a halt. Pluschow had again fallen victim to the fickle River Thames. With almost lightning rapidity, the tide had ebbed. He was stuck fast in a boat full of water. Despair mingled with anger, and frustration overcame him. It seemed that although he had outwitted all those who sought to recapture him, the old Thames was to hold him prisoner.

The stench of the oozing black slime on which the boat now sat reached his nose. He knew from his observations of the tidal flow on previous nights that the water would not rise again until the following afternoon. He certainly could not wait till then, for he would be exposed for all to see. Somehow he had to extricate himself. He was several yards away from dry land and he wrestled with the problem of how he was to reach it. The boat-hook, a long pole with a curved hook at one end, looked like his only hope of salvation. He estimated that, with luck, he might be able to vault the distance between the boat and the shore. It was his only chance.

He braced himself for the leap, raised the boat-hook, thrust it into the mud and threw himself forward. Alas, the point of the boat-hook sank into the oozing quagmire and Pluschow's vault dropped him far short of the target. He fell amid the morass of slime with a squelching flop that seemed to resound across the shore and must alert the sentry – but the even pad of the soldier's feet continued.

Pluschow willed himself not to fight the mud, for struggle must inevitably suck him deeper into it. Composing himself he rose and step by step made the short distance to the shore, covered in a thick coating of malodorous slime. Pluschow's ordeal had gone unheard by the 'vigilant' guardian.

There seemed to Pluschow little point in attempting to sneak past the sentry who at this time was stationary on a small bridge over which the escaper would have to cross. Pluschow resolved to attempt the bold approach.

After scraping as much of the congealed mud as he could off his clothes, he proceded towards the bridge. Over these past few days Pluschow had acquired some considerable skill as an actor and now he summoned all of it to take on the wobbling gait of a drunk. He staggered towards the sentry, wavering in his walk and humming a nondescript ballad. As he drew closer to the soldier he raised an arm in drunken greeting. The bridge was narrow and collision with the soldier was inevitable. Pluschow bumped against him and in slurred tones made an unintelligible apology. The sentry smiled, much to Pluschow's relief.

'One over the eight, eh, mate?' the soldier asked.

'Thass right, general,' Pluschow mumbled.

'Go on. On you go,' the soldier said, patting Pluschow on his way over the bridge.

'Blimey! I wouldn't fancy havin' 'is 'ead in the mornin',' the sentry thought aloud, in a humorous cockney drawl.

Pluschow staggered on until he reckoned he was well out of sight of the sentry then he glanced around, just to confirm that he could not be seen. In that instant, he 'sobered up' and quickly made his way down to the shore.

On the pebbly beach he stripped off his clothes, and tucked away his meagre possessions as he had done before. This time he would attempt to swim out to the boats he could see not far offshore and 'borrow' one to row out to the steamer. The river was oily calm but there was an ominous phosphorescence about it which troubled Pluschow since it shone when the water was disturbed. Snake-like he slid into the water, trying desperately not to disturb its flatness, and struck out towards the small boats. All went well until he was caught by a current, the same one which had dashed his hopes the other night. He fought against it and at last gained the first of the rowing boats. Gathering all the strength he could muster he hoisted himself on board, only to find that the small craft carried no oars. Disheartened, Pluschow slid back into the water and made his way to a second boat. It too was devoid of oars. So too with the third and all the others he tried. Not a single one had oars on board. It was no good; he had to give up and strike back to the shore.

With heavy, dejected strokes, he swam back to the shore and took a wide detour back to the wood-pile. His whole body shook with cold but exhaustion won the battle and he lapsed into a shallow sleep. Some hours later he woke with a start. There was someone rummaging around the wood-pile. The sky was bright. He had overslept. The owner of the wood-yard had already arrived and was about his business. Pluschow peered anxiously through a gap in a stack of wood. He could see the elderly man inspecting his wares. He turned and looked in Pluschow's direction, staring directly at the wood-pile behind which the fugitive hid. Pluschow was transfixed, riveted to the spot. Surely he must be seen. He could feel the man's eyes penetrating the stack of wood but then he turned and walked away, heading for a hut nearby. When he had disappeared inside, Pluschow crept out of the yard and made haste away from the shore. He had had enough excitement for one night.

He wandered into London, whiling away the hours of day-light and in the course of it visiting a matinée at a small theatre. He could barely raise a grin at the comic antics of the performers on stage. But when, as a finale, a special feature depicting the defeat of the Huns in the trenches of France was enacted, his determination was roused to a new peak. He shouldered his way through the audience standing at the back of the auditorium and left the theatre. That visit to the theatre had cost him his last pound. Now he was penniless. By whatever means he could find, he had to escape – he could last no longer in London.

Back he went to the river, following its course along the south bank, scouring it for some small craft which would take him out to a steamer moored in mid-stream. On his travels he discovered a scull which he purloined and carried until he reached Gravesend, where he found the answer to his prayers. By the beach was a small patch of grass which led down to the shore-line. Upon that grass lay a man and woman, with their children utterly oblivious to the 'tramp' who meandered on to their patch. Loosely tied up at the shore was a dinghy which they had used to bring them to their picnic place. Pluschow decided that dinghy would be his. It was getting dark as he casually made his way towards the little craft and untied her. None of the family romping in the dwindling light noticed him and with a deft push on the scull the boat was slipping out into the river. It was equipped with sculls and he dipped them into the water and pulled well out into the main stream. No cries of alarm came from the shore.

The tide was on the ebb and despite Pluschow's powerful strokes, he was drawn towards some fishing-boats moored not far offshore. The dinghy, of its own will, lazily bumped against one of the fishing-boats and traversed its beam. It was a nervous moment for the German. On deck a young mother nursed her baby, humming a lullaby. She took the bump of the dinghy off the boat to be one of the many sounds of the river and continued her song. Soon Pluschow was past the boat and pulling out to mid-stream but now he was caught in the full force of the cur-rent and it drove him down river at speed, despite his efforts to arrest its race. Ahead lay a pontoon bridge which spanned the river and on it he could make out the shapes of patrolling sol-diers. There was no avoiding it. He would simply have to brazen it out.

The dinghy swept boldly on as the current thrust it forward while Pluschow did his best to steer it. The dinghy rocketed through the gap between the two pontoons supporting the bridge but as it did so, there were challenging yells from the soldiers. Pluschow ignored them as the boat appeared at the other side of the bridge and careered on, oblivious to the prospect of a bullet in the back, but it did not come.

The fierce current gripped the tiny craft and hauled her down-river. She was now all but uncontrollable and the pitch darkness that lay ahead seemed as if the boat were being cast into a black hell. Then suddenly a towering collier loomed large ahead with its anchor cable in Pluschow's path. Pluschow grabbed his boat's painter and threw it around the cable. The dinghy almost capsized but by the skilled use of his spread feet, Pluschow succeeded in keeping her afloat.

Panting, Pluschow secured the painter to the cable and caught his breath. He rested for a few moments then glanced off to his right where he could see the outline of a steamer – *his* steamer, one of the Dutch ships which daily plied the route between London and Flushing. She was his target but he would have to wait until the force of the tide subsided. He simply did not have the strength to fight the flow of the river.

Pluschow waited – and waited. Hours passed but still the Thames rushed by like a race. The first light of dawn brought an eeriness to the scene, giving the great hulking ships that lay moored in the river an almost ghost-like appearance. But still the river dashed by unabated. He realised then that he would never make it across to the Dutch steamer. Soon it would be daylight and that would bring the menace of discovery. Again he would have to give up.

Pluschow released the painter and the dinghy moved away from the collier. She drifted downstream until at last the German was able to guide her to the shore. He had missed yet another chance but now he had a boat which he could use the following night to get himself out to a steamer.

In the meantime he had to hide up and that was more diffi-cult than before, for he had to secrete the boat as well as himself. But he found the ideal place, a dilapidated old bridge, so rotted that it was clearly no longer used. He pushed the dinghy under-neath to a position where it could be seen from neither the river nor the land and secured it there. Then he took the sculls and retreated inshore to find himself a suitable hiding-place to await the hour of departure.

For sixteen hours he lay there, not daring to move, trembling but in high spirits. Night came and he chose his moment. He launched his dinghy into the river when the tide was coming in. Pluschow pulled the craft out into the flow and as it became caught in the water's grip it needed little effort for him to take her upstream.

It was a little after eight in the evening and the flow of the incoming tide bore the dinghy upstream with it. An hour passed and he could see ahead of him the collier to which he had been tethered the night before. Again he caught the anchor chain and made fast to it, there to bide his time until all was quiet aboard the Dutch steamer which lay off to starboard and slightly downstream.

After midnight Pluschow cast off from the collier and rowed the short distance to the steamer, which he now recognised as the *Princess Juliana*.

His eyes scanned the Dutch ship as he drew closer. No lights showed and she was silent, but even so he knew that there would be a watch.

Silently he dipped the sculls into the water and manoeuvred the dinghy alongside the buoy to which the steamer was held fast by a thick hawser. His movements were cat-like as he grabbed the thick hawser and abandoned the dinghy. In that move he gave the little craft which had borne him to his goal a sharp kick and she drifted off down-river.

Pluschow clung to the hawser for a few moments, mentally and physically summoning the strength to scale it. Then hand-over-hand and with his feet wrapped around it he began to scale it, his ears primed for any sound that might betray the presence of someone out of his view on the ship that loomed above him. No sound came, only the ripple of water.

Finally he reached the top and peered on to the deck. The forecastle was deserted. Perfect. In a moment he was on deck and hiding behind the windlass, waiting, listening and watching, planning his next move.

Pluschow removed his boots and in his stocking-feet crept along the deck. Then he stopped dead in his tracks. He could hear voices. He slipped into the dark shadows by his side and peered astern. Beneath him he could see two men on the cargo deck. His target was the usual one for a stowaway – a lifeboat – but to reach one of these he would have to pass the men on the deck. Then luck played a merciful part. Two women passengers came on deck and engaged the men in conversation. Pluschow saw his chance and he slid along the opposite side of the deck until he came to a lifeboat. He undid the ropes on the outboard side of the lifeboat, slipped through the gap into blackness and pulled back the boat's cover. Pluschow rolled himself into a tight ball in the well of the lifeboat and within minutes was fast asleep.

The blast of the ship's siren made Pluschow sit bolt upright, wakened instantly from his sleep. In these first moments of consciousness he was bewildered and had difficulty in working out where he was. Cautiously, he eased up the cover which spread over the lifeboat and chanced a glance outside. It was broad daylight. His eyes, unaccustomed to the brightness took a few seconds to focus but when they did they widened in disbelief. The *Princess Juliana* was nosing gently and serenely into the harbour at Flushing in Holland. Pluschow had slept through his flight to freedom.

Overwhelmed with delight, he took out his knife, ripped a gaping hole in the life-boat cover and stood up. He did not care a damn now who saw him. It was his intention to give himself up to the ship's captain. But the decks were crammed with passengers and crew milling about, waiting to disembark. No one paid any attention to him. In a strange sort of way, he was disappointed. There he was, having escaped from England and no one seemed to care.

Pluschow emerged on to the deck where the gangway was being lowered to the pier. Soon the gangway was crammed with passengers rushing to get off and crewmen obediently carrying luggage. Pluschow joined them and in less than a minute was on dry land. He saw the passengers making their way in a throng towards the passport control and it was then that the fear of possible internment came back to him.

Pluschow mingled with the crowd, looking around for a way to avoid the check-point. Then he saw it; a door marked clearly with a warning that exit through it was forbidden. Again no one seemed to be paying any attention to him so he sidled up to it, turned the handle and much to his surprise, it opened. One step forward, and he was in Holland. Free! . . . Or at least partly free. He had still to reach the Fatherland.

It was not long before Pluschow made contact with two Germans who fed him and gave him the most luxurious bath he had ever had. Then with money supplied by them, he boarded a train for Germany.

The train had barely left the station when a plain clothes detective collared Pluschow and demanded to see his papers. The detective explained that he was from the security police and that this was merely a routine check. Of all the people to ask, he had to chose Pluschow. The German realised that he had no alternative but to own up and he recounted his story to the Dutch policeman who, astonishing as the story was, accepted it as true. When the train finally reached the German border, the frontier police there were less easily convinced. Without papers of any sort or any means of identification, Pluschow was arrested under suspicion of being a spy! Here he was, having travelled many thousands of miles to fight for the Kaiser, standing accused of being a spy. He could not believe it.

But Lieutenant Gunther Pluschow need not have concerned himself. His real identity was soon proved and he was acclaimed a hero. Pluschow, the only man ever to escape from a British prisoner of war camp in England and return to Germany, was awarded the Iron Cross First Class by the Kaiser himself.

Pluschow survived the war and his spirit of adventure remained in time of peace. In the late 1920s he set out to explore the unmapped areas of South America, using an aeroplane to get a bird's-eye view of that mighty continent. But in 1931, while flying through a mountainous region, his aircraft crashed. This time for Gunther Pluschow, perhaps the most successful German escaper of the two world wars, there was no escape.

2

The Aces

Albert Ball drew the bow across the strings of his violin in gentle, caressing strokes while the fingers of his left hand found the notes and rocked in vibrato, bringing a round, resonant tone to the slow, melancholy tune he played. His slender, angular face tilted sideways, his chin holding the instrument firmly between it and his shoulder. His dark eyes reflected the mood of the sombre, almost dirge-like music that came from the violin. He walked as he played, not upon the boards of the concert stage but across a grassy field in northern France. He strolled aimlessly, careless of his course, his mind oblivious to all but the music – yet, a scant few miles from where he walked, one of the bloodiest battles of the First World War was being fought. It was 1917. Men were dying by the thousand under the weight of a German artillery bombardment. Albert Ball knew none of it, although the ground beneath his feet reverberated and shook as shell after shell thudded into it not far away, gouging vast craters out of the French countryside.

The crashing roar of the battle was but the orchestral accompaniment to the soloist's performance, the timpany that complemented the performance. In the brief interlude all was music to him. He was alone with his violin and from that he could conjure beauty in sound and escape, if only briefly, from the war.

The melody ended. Ball took the violin from his shoulder. In that instant he was back to reality. He looked towards the front line, only a few miles distant. The sky was heavy and foreboding as if the heavens knew of the carnage. Every other second, the low dark cloud was lit by the orange flash of gunfire and explosion as another shell was hurtled towards the soldiers crouching in their trenches.

Ball turned away from it and headed towards a long line of tents at the edge of the wide field. In front of them stood a group of Nieuport Scout fighters, single-seater aircraft, frail, string and canvas aeroplanes armed with a single machine-gun.

His stride was slow and lethargic as he reflected upon the futility of the war. A devout Christian, Ball hated this awful conflict. He was in his early twenties when he was cast like so many others into the holocaust. There was as great a conflict in his own mind as there was in these bloody trenches or in the furious dog-fights that raged in the sky above them. Ball, the music-lover, the Christian, the remote introvert who preferred his own company to that of others; Ball, the loner who shunned the wild parties, the bouts of drinking and womanising his comrades indulged in to escape the horror and the fear of death. How could such a man reconcile his inherent pacifism with killing his fellow-man in aerial clinches high above the trenches? His mind was in a torment, torn between duty to his country and his Christian goodwill toward men. He was an enigmatic youngster, deep and intense, struggling within himself for the answer to that paramount problem. If anything, he found his answer in God. It became his belief that it was the will of the Almighty that he should be a fighter pilot. He had a conviction that the Lord would protect him and it must have been this that drove Albert Ball on to become the first of the great British fighter aces.

Ball fought in the sky with a ferocity, dash and daring unsurpassed by any other fighter pilot then or since. Quiet and subdued on the ground, this slim young man underwent a strange metamorphosis when he took to the air. He fought like a demon. He knew no caution and was oblivious to danger. He was a hunter and killer without peer; a strange, almost mysterious man whom no one knew intimately but everyone respected – even his enemies. For a time Ball was the ace of aces, the top-scoring fighter pilot of the Royal Flying Corps. But not so long before few would have believed that he would even qualify as a pilot . . .

Born in Nottingham in 1896, Ball was the son of one of the city's most prominent civic leaders who later became Mayor. Albert was shy and detached with a ready smile which endeared him to those he met but with a distant look in his round brown eyes. He disliked school and his academic achievements left much to be be desired. He had a passion for all things mechanical and even as a young boy acquired a not inconsiderable skill in repairing the primitive motor engines of the day. Some years later this mechanical mastery was to save his life.

In the meanwhile, Albert found a second love – guns. He acquired a considerable collection of hand guns and at the age of ten was an accomplished shot. He practised regularly out of harm's way on a secluded tennis court where he set up targets. It was alien to his nature to shoot birds and he was quite content to blast away both at static and improvised moving targets. Through this he developed a keen eye and fast reactions and became a crack shot.

Ball had barely time to recover from school when Europe was plunged into war. The call to arms came and he dutifully answered by enlisting in the Sherwood Foresters, a locally-raised and famous regiment. Ball could hardly have been said to be itching to get into the scrap with the Hun. History lessons at Trent College public school had not fired him with interest in Britain's glorious warlike past. It was therefore with some relief that he found himself posted to a cyclist unit near Ealing on the outskirts of London. If pedalling a bike was to be his contribution to the war effort then he was quite content with that.

But while he was stationed at Ealing he first caught sight of an aeroplane in flight. The erratic drone of its engine reached his ears as he pedalled along the road. He glanced skyward and with wobbling wheels saw this mechanical bird wing its way over his head. Ball dismounted and watched in awe. She was truly a marvel to behold. How, he pondered, could a fragile winged machine, barely covered with canvas, a mass of struts and wires, bear a man through the air?

The drone of the engine died but Ball stood transfixed, still gaping at the machine as it slowly disappeared from view. In the moments that it had taken that aircraft to overfly the cyclist, Albert Ball had made a decision: he resolved there and then to become a flier.

It was an excited young cyclist who rode back to his camp that day and began making enquiries as to how he should become a pilot in Britain's embryonic air force, the Royal Flying Corps. In his innocence, he believed that he had nothing else to do but apply for a transfer to the RFC whereupon he would train to become the pilot of one of their brand-new machines. His hopes and expectations were very quickly dashed. The Army had other plans for Albert. They were quite happy with their cyclist and content to leave things much the way they were. The British High Command viewed the new-fangled flying machine with much scepticism. It must be remembered that in the wars of the past, the cavalry charge, the sabre, lance, musket and bayonet had been the deciding factors in battle. The generals who commanded Britain's army were of the old school; text-book soldiers, entrenched in their tactics and strategy, like im-movable objects. Albert Ball resolved to push them aside, out of his way, for he had made up his mind to fly.

There did, however, stand in his way a force perhaps infinitely more formidable than the generals – Private Ball's Company Sergeant Major, a bull-necked tyrant who, although not much taller than Ball himself, assumed the proportions of a giant by virtue of a stentorian voice which could make a parade ground tremble.

It took no little courage on Ball's part to face up to the Sergeant Major and request a transfer to the RFC.

The CSM's eyes bulged from their sockets. For a moment Ball thought he was about to become the target of the CSM's pace stick. Instead he exploded verbally . . .

'Do *what?*' he roared. 'You want to do what, my lad?'

'I want to fly with the Royal . . .' Ball began, but the CSM opened fire with a thundering verbal volley.

'Don't answer back!' the CSM barked, his face a mere two inches from Ball's and glowing crimson. His knuckles shone white as he gripped his pace stick. There was a pause, an ominous one, in which the Sergeant Major seemed to be con-sidering whether the trembling private who stood before him had gone mad or was trying to 'work his ticket', by feigning insanity. After all, by the sergeant major's reckoning, only a lunatic would take to the air in a flying machine.

'Are you up to something, laddie?' he said with a distinct tone of suspicion in his voice. 'Tryin' to work yer ticket are you? Got a touch of the jitters in case we're sent off to France, into the trenches. Frightened o' a bit o' cold steel?'

'No, sergeant . . .' Ball interjected meekly.

'You know, my son, I got a deep feelin' in my bones that we

have here a hero wot does not want to be a hero.'

This inferred reflection upon his moral fibre brought a unique glare to Ball's eyes. Mild-mannered he may have been, but Ball was imbued with a singlemindedness that now shone in his eyes. The CSM saw it and his 'bark' subsided. He was no fool. He had been badgering and disciplining men for years but he had the sense to recognise when he was on a losing wicket. His tune changed.

Ball's stare was fixed – straight into the eyes of his baiter. The CSM not wishing to admit defeat turned to mockery.

'Well then, laddie, if you want to risk your flamin' neck in one of them flyin' coffins, you go ahead an' learn to fly – but you'll do it in your own time, see? And at your own expense. You ain't wastin' the army's money or time.'

Ball had won but there was to be a hard slog ahead of him. His only 'free time' was after lights out at night and before parade early in the morning. Somehow or other he would have to squeeze his flying lessons in early in the morning and on his very infrequent days off. There was, too, another problem – money. He would have to pay for his flying lessons out of his own pocket and they were not cheap. In those early days of the war, the RFC wanted only qualified pilots, prepared to foot the bill for their training out of their own pockets. Ball's bank balance was low – but his determination was high and so it was that he enrolled as a student pilot at the Hendon flying school.

Day after day at dawn, Ball pedalled to Hendon for a quick flying lesson, then back to Ealing for the parade. It was a bleary-eyed youth who presented himself on parade and his condition incurred the displeasure of the CSM. But although volubly voicing this displeasure, the sergeant grew to have a sneaking admiration for the would-be aviator.

However, doubt was creeping into Ball's mind. His lessons were nightmares. He was no natural flier and disaster was only just averted on more than one occasion. The sky was clearly not his natural element or so it seemed at the time. His progress was slow and his take-offs and landings hair-raising both to watch and to experience. The knack of flying an aeroplane had not yet clicked. He had not yet got the fine touch required of the pilot to put the aeroplane safely back down on the ground in one piece after a circuit or so of the airfield. It was a deal of time in coming. But he had determination and faith even if his instructor did not share it. When he finally flew solo, the instructor hardly dared watch but Ball performed a near perfect touchdown. He was beside himself with joy. Now he eagerly looked forward to the day when he would gain his wings. But there were to be many near tragedies before that morning of 26 January 1916 when he stood rigidly to attention while the coveted cloth wings were pinned to his left breast. After much trial, Albert Ball had become a pilot. The RFC had gained a pilot of dubious skill, while the Army had lost an intrepid cyclist.

Ball, now a lieutenant in the RFC, went to war a month later. At least, he went to France, and at an airfield well behind the Allied lines gave his new squadron commander a stunning display in how to commit suicide by flying. Major Marsh, the commander of 13 Squadron to which Ball had been sent, found difficulty in believing his eyes. By some miracle – surely by divine intervention – Ball managed to land his machine in 'classic' style, approaching the field at a crazy angle, levelling off for touch-down a split second before the wheels *hit* the ground then bumping along the grass in a series of kangaroo hops until finally coming to rest.

Lieutenant Ball's feet had not touched the ground before an anxious airman informed him that Major Marsh wanted him in his tent immediately. The young pilot had an idea of what might be coming.

Marsh glowered at him as he pulled back the tent flap. Ball entered and saluted.

'Never!' Marsh began, 'Never have I seen flying like it. Not even the rawest student flies an aeroplane like that. *I* couldn't even if I tried! How you got down alive defies explanation. Ball, I can't afford to have a pilot like you in my squadron. Aircraft are scarce and the way you fly, you'd be writing them off daily – and yourself with them. I have no alternative but to recommend that you be sent back to England for further training. That's all. You can go.'

'But, sir!' Ball began.

'No buts, Ball!' Marsh commanded. 'My mind is made up.'

Ball left the tent. He had failed miserably. He would suffer the humiliation of returning to England from the war in France without having fired a single shot. But there was a remote ray of hope. Marsh could not send him back before certain formalities had been completed. For once, the notorious 'red tape' was to play in Ball's favour.

Before Marsh could put his threat into action, it was Ball's turn as an operational pilot to take off on a reconnaissance mission over the German lines. He resolved then that he would prove to Marsh that he had what it took to be a pilot.

The aircraft in which he was to undertake the mission was a BE2c scout, a two-seater aeroplane in which Ball, the pilot, sat in the front cockpit and his observer, who manned the machine-gun, sat in the rear cockpit. Both cockpits were open to the elements and decidedly draughty. The BE2c was not a fighter but was designed as a reconnaissance aeroplane. It was a difficult aircraft to handle, and like most other aircraft of the time, it was flimsy, built of wood and covered with almost paper-thin stretched canvas. It had the appearance of a craft which would disintegrate if caught the wrong way by a strong gust of wind. Aerobatics in an aeroplane like this were out of the question. It could stand up to little or no strain on its airframe, so straight and level flight was about its limit. The BE2c was certainly no match for the German fighters, notably the Fokkers with their fixed forward-firing machine-guns and good manoeuvrability. The Fokkers could fly rings round the clumsy reconnaissance planes and BE2cs fell victim to them at an alarming rate, earning for themselves the accolade of 'Fokker fodder'.

Undaunted by the inadequacy of his mount, Ball took off with a none-too-happy observer sitting behind him, and joined the formation of reconnaissance aircraft droning towards the German lines.

For the first time since he had arrived in France, Ball saw for himself the trenches of the front. He was aghast at the devastation below. The whole area for as far as the eye could see had the appearance of a lunar landscape, pock-marked by huge craters and a cobweb pattern of trench systems. The defoliated trees, stripped of their branches and leaves by the shelling, stood stark and gaunt, like embers. Shell-holes full of rainwater were lethal pools for unwary soldiers. Mud was everywhere. The sight brought a wave of nausea over the young pilot. What awful horrors there must be down there, he thought, thankful that he would fight his battle away from that.

The BE2c rocked as she was caught by crosswinds and Ball had to jockey her into position in the formation as she swept on over the lines. At last he was over enemy territory. Now he could expect action. The Germans rarely ventured across the British lines, in case they were shot down in hostile territory. They preferred to wait for their prey behind their own door. The British squadrons were more adventurous ... and as a result were more likely to lose their pilots to German prisoner of war camps, that is, if they were fortunate enough to survive an encounter.

Ball's nerves were taut as he scanned the sky above, below and in front of him while his observer kept watch on their tail. There was a faint feeling of security tucked away as he was in the middle of the formation but he had been warned of the cunning of the Hun and no one was safe behind the German lines, least of all in a lumbering aircraft like his.

The attack came like a thunderbolt. The formation of aircraft was at one moment cruising unmolested; in the next, the leader was frantically waving his arm in the air, the warning that an attack was imminent. Ball looked around then he saw them: tiny specks tumbling down out of a high cloud and growing into the unmistakable shapes of Hun fighters.

The British aircraft broke formation, scattering in all directions while flashes from the German guns brought streams of bullets zipping down amid the mêlée of British biplanes. Ball's aircraft rocked as his observer unleashed a burst of fire at a fighter which plummeted down through the aeroplanes as they bolted. Ball banked violently and the observer's bullets went far wide of the mark. He cast a sideways glance just in time to see another BE2c raked by fire from a German fighter. It seemed to stop in its flight path for a moment, pause, nose up, then drop like a stone to the ground in a curious slow motion. As it spun downwards, a flame flickered up from the petrol tank, and in an instant the whole aeroplane was enveloped in a vast ball of fire. Both pilot and observer suffered the most feared fate of the fighter pilot to go down in flames, roasted alive before the seal of death came when the aircraft shattered on the ground.

Ball had no time for sentiment, no time to feel pity, sorrow or even revulsion at the sight. He would see it many more times but now he had himself, his observer and his own aircraft to think of. Only brief seconds had elapsed since the attack had begun. He wheeled the BE2c around in a wide arc, seeking out Germans but they were gone. The sky was empty. No other aircraft was in sight. Neither friend nor foe. This was one of the curious phenomena of the aerial 'dog-fights', as these skirmishes were known. It was common for a battle to rage for less than a minute, then for the sky to be deserted.

By now, Ball was deep inside enemy territory. There was no aircraft with which to do battle. Now was the time to go home. He brought the BE2c round and set her on a course back over the lines. But Ball's keen ear detected a change in the note of the engine. Something was wrong. His fears were confirmed when the engine gave a tubercular cough, then spluttered and spat. The propeller in front of him faltered in its gyration then suddenly stopped and jammed rigidly, defiantly, despite the pilot's effort to goad the engine into restarting.

Ball circled, trying to maintain height and find a landing-place. Luck was with him. Below lay a field, one of the few in that expanse of country which had not suffered from shell-fire.

He yelled back to his observer.

'I'm going to put her down in that field. Hang on to your hat. It's going to be a tough one.'

Had he looked back, Ball would have seen the expression of horror on the face of his observer. The poor man knew of his pilot's reputation as a flier and now he was about to put a crippled aeroplane down on a bumpy field – and behind the enemy lines at that. The observer clung to the rim of the cockpit for dear life as the BE2c swept nearer and nearer to the ground. It won't be long now, he thought, closing his eyes and expecting to be torn to pieces in the crash.

Ball's eyes were intent upon the field. It was rough and un-even – and on the short side, especially for one of *his* landings. Soon the ground was a blur, then the wheels touched. The aircraft bumped and cavorted across the field mercifully coming to rest a few feet from a hedgerow. Ball heaved a sigh of relief while his observer gaped in amazement. They had made it.

Both men scrambled out of the machine, dropped to the ground and scurried for the cover of the nearby hedgerow. Huddled there, both with pistols drawn, they furtively looked around, watching for the field-grey uniforms of the enemy. But all was quiet. No sign of a German soldier. At the slightest hint of an intruder, Ball would have to put a bullet into the fuel tank of the aircraft. He dared not let it fall into the hands of the enemy, but it appeared that they had landed unseen.

Gingerly they crept out of hiding and after scouting the surrounding area, Ball put his mechanical expertise to work. After some time, he found the cause of the problem but by then darkness was closing in. He could not work on the engine without light so both men decided to bed down in their respective cockpits.

Sleep was sporadic that night. The bitter cold numbed their limbs and when dawn came and Ball set to repair the engine he had difficulty in bringing the magic touch to his frozen fingers, but at last it came and a throw of the propeller brought the engine bursting into life. Now they had to move fast. They had arrived in the field silently the previous night and this must have had something to do with their not being spotted by the enemy but now with the engine roaring they had to get out fast.

Ball pushed forward the throttle and the BE2c picked up speed. A gentle pull back on the joystick and she was airborne – but only just. The fixed undercarriage collected a clump of hedgerow as the aircraft skimmed over the edge of the field and climbed away towards the British lines. But their troubles were far from over. Before the British lines came into view, a freak storm blew up with startling suddenness. Blinding snow forced Ball to ground level. He found a level piece of land and down he went, settling gently upon a thin coating of white snow.

Neither he nor his observer could do anything but wait until the storm had passed. Luckily it did not last long. Luckier still, it had forced the Germans to take cover, so again the aeroplane was not spotted.

Finally, the sky cleared. Ball turned the BE2c into the wind and was soon airborne. It was eight o'clock when the aeroplane finally touched down at its home base. Both men slumped exhausted in their cockpits, drawing breath before hauling themselves out and jumping to the ground. It was then that Ball spotted a familiar figure striding purposefully towards him. It was Marsh.

'Well,' Ball said to his observer, 'now for the crunch.'

But as Marsh drew nearer, Ball thought he could discern a hint of a smile on the commander's face. It couldn't be possible, he thought. Marsh's pace quickened until he was trotting and finally reached Ball. He *was* smiling.

'Well done, Ball,' he said, grabbing the young pilot's hand and pumping it vigorously. Ball's jaw fell in stunned amazement.

'We'd given you up for a goner. Frankly, old chap, I didn't think you had it in you to bring the old crate back in one piece. Seems I was mistaken. You've got the spirit we need – bags of guts and determination. Maybe we'll make a pilot of you yet. I think you can forget about your trip back to England now. We'll lick you into shape here.'

With that Marsh turned on his heels and was gone.

It took Ball a few moments to recover from this revelation but when he did, he could merely stammer, 'Well I'll be jiggered!'

Ball's experience and the change in attitude of his squadron commander had a marked effect upon him. The confidence he had lacked came to him and there was a notable improvement in his flying. But he had yet to show his teeth in battle and within himself he knew that only then would he be able to decide for himself whether or not he would make a pilot.

That day of decision came on 28 March 1916 when he and Lieutenant Villiers, his observer, were on an artillery spotting mission over the enemy lines. Ball's BE2c was crossing Givenchy, a town behind the Hun lines when Ball saw them: two German aircraft flying at about 5000 feet a few miles away. He yelled to Villiers.

'Cock that gun of yours, Villiers. We've got company. I'm going into the attack.'

With that he swung the aircraft round and headed towards the Germans who were flying wing-tip to wing-tip. Ball's engine roared as he thrust forward the throttle and charged in for the attack. So far he had not been seen by the Germans but as they caught sight of the BE2c, they broke formation. Ball selected his prey and dived in to the attack. Villiers behind him unleashed a withering hail of bullets which sprayed the German machine, without any apparent effect, but perforating the canvas covering the fuselage. He cursed as his machine-gun chattered. The enemy plane was made of stout stuff and refused to succumb.

Determined to give Villiers the best chance of a kill, Ball held the BE2c steady on her course but, in a flash, bullets whipped past his head. He had not noticed that the Germans' companion had manoeuvred himself on to their tail and was pumping lead his way. Still Ball held his aircraft steady, careless of the thread of bullets that zipped past his machine until the target German aircraft lurched as the pilot was riddled by Ball's shells. The plane winged over and hurtled earthwards in a death dive. Only then, when the victory was secure did Ball jink out of the way of his attacker and take evasive action, rolling away from the fusillade of bullets.

The remaining German pilot, seeing his prey slip away and aware of the fate of his comrade, prudently turned tail and headed for home. There was no hope of catching him, Ball knew. His aircraft was more powerful and could outrun the BE2c with ease. Jubilant, Ball and Villiers headed for home.

But although elated at his success, Ball's victory was tinged with disappointment. He felt sure that, had he been on his own, without his observer to consider, and in a more manoeuvrable aircraft, he would have taken greater risks and could have shot down both aircraft. He felt that reconnaissance flying was tame stuff and longed to try his hand at flying a fighter.

He knew that there was a single-seater Bristol fighter attached to the squadron and he itched to try it out. He went to see Marsh.

At first Marsh would hear nothing of it. Despite Ball's recent success, he felt sure that the young pilot did not have the flying skill to handle a fighter. But Ball persisted and eventually Marsh relented. Permission was reluctantly granted for Ball to do some 'circuits and bumps' in the Bristol fighter. At that, Ball raced out on to the grass field and found the fighter. For a few moments, he stood back from it, his eyes tracing its trim lines. She was superb, a miracle of design, in Ball's mind, sleek, slender, lithe and from nose to tail the fighter.

Almost absentmindedly, Ball ran his finger tips along the leading edge of her wings. She was a thing of beauty. Mounted upon her engine cowling was a single forward-firing machine-gun, which, by being synchronised with the engine and the rotating propeller, fired forward between the blades. One simply had to point the aircraft at the target and fire. No observer to worry about. Here was the fighter aircraft in which the pilot was both chauffeur and fighter.

Ball knew even before he climbed into the single cockpit that he had found his mount. As he started the engine he could feel the whole aircraft surge with power. He too trembled with excitement. For the first time in his short flying career, he felt at one with the aeroplane, an integral part, as if a new partnership had been formed.

The sensation of speed as the Bristol shot along the grass was both frightening and exhilarating. In no time, the Bristol was in the air, sweeping skyward, the ground receding beneath Ball. Up she went, almost effortlessly, soaring into a sky, clear and blue, spotted only by puffy, white cumulus. No longer was Ball the fledgeling. A marriage had been made and was about to be consummated in a display of aerobatics which left the watchers on the ground speechless. Gone were Ball's inhibitions. He handled the Bristol Scout with the skill and fearless abandon of a seasoned veteran.

He fought a simulated battle with the scattered clouds in the sky, attacking them, thrusting headlong into them, momentarily blinded by their mist then emerging to find further fluffy prey. He looped, rolled, banked, dived and spun in sheer delight at flying this aeroplane. Topping ninety miles an hour, he rocketed over the airfield, shaking the tents at its edge in the draught of his pass. Then he landed, a different man from the one who had taken to the air a short while before. Ball was a fighter pilot. He knew it and no one who had witnessed that dazzling display of airmanship could deny it.

But fate was to play a cruel hand in Ball's immediate future. A fellow pilot took the Bristol, the squadron's one and only fighter aircraft, for a spin and crashed it, denying Ball the opportunity of becoming more familiar with it.

A week later, however, another Bristol Scout arrived, fresh from the factory in England. Ball claimed it immediately and was airborne within hours of its arrival. He tried a few man-oeuvres then cocked the gun in front of him, to get the feel of firing it in flight. He curled his finger around the trigger and squeezed. The propeller in front of him disintegrated into a thousand bits as the bullets shattered it. Razor-sharp splinters shot back at the cockpit and Ball was saved only by the small windscreen in front of him. The synchronising mechanism was faulty; the bullets had hit the propeller blades, instead of passing harmlessly between them. The engine roared in a screeching crescendo as it raced, now without the propeller which was but a stump. For a few moments the aircraft continued forward, driven on by the impetus but, without a propeller to give it its thrust, it began to sink. The shock of the mishap caught Ball unawares and he had dropped a few hundred feet before he succeeded in regaining some semblance of control. He switched off the engine and all was silence. Luckily he was within gliding distance of the airfield and Ball brought the Bristol Scout safely down. The experience had been alarming but it in no way dulled his enthusiasm for becoming a fighter pilot. There was but one way of achieving this aim and that was by getting a transfer to a fighter squadron. His career as a reconnaissance pilot had been unimpressive and he used this as a lever with which to persuade Marsh to recommend his transfer.

On 7 May 1916, Ball bade his squadron goodbye and left to join Number 11 fighter squadron where, for the first time, he was 'introduced' to the Nieuport Scout fighter aircraft. The Nieuport Scout was a small single-seat biplane of French design powered by a big, 110 horse-power Le Rhône nine-cylinder air-cooled engine driving a two-bladed propeller. Like its contemporaries, it had a wooden framework covered by stretched fabric, but it had one distinct advantage over other biplanes. The lower set of wings was narrower than the upper set, which gave the pilot a good view downwards and allowed him better vision in battle if he came under attack from below. Mounted on the centrepiece of the upper wings was a Lewis machine-gun with a rapid rate of fire.

The Nieuport could out-pace and out-manoeuvre the Bristol and indeed most of the enemy fighter aircraft. Ball had found the ultimate in fighters. Between them, he and the Nieuport were to subtract a sizeable chunk from the fighter strength of the German Air Service.

Within days Ball was in action, throwing himself into the battle with an abandon which terrified the Germans and left his comrades aghast. Before many weeks had passed he was already a legendary figure. He flew alone and would fly headlong into enemy formations, utterly careless of the opposition, the greater the number of aircraft he faced, the more brazen he became in his attack. The sheer boldness of his methods reaped rewards and his score of kills mounted.

Ball would charge nose-to-nose towards an enemy, firing as he went until the enemy either disintegrated or broke away. To make sure that Germans knew just whom they were facing when he bounded out of the sky at them, he attached a bright red spinner to the hub of his propeller and it was not very long before the Germans were fleeing for their lives at the very sight of the red-nosed aircraft.

The risks Ball took were such that in the first few weeks of his career as a fighter pilot he was shot down no fewer than six times but on every single occasion he landed his machine on the British side of the lines, so that it could be repaired and flown again. His energy was limitless. On one occasion, he returned to his base covered from head to toe in thick black oil and with the Nieuport's fuselage ripped apart by bullet holes. The elevator controls were shot to pieces. Without hesitation he wiped his face with a rag, made his own repairs to the aircraft and in no time at all was airborne again and back in the fray.

Ball's mastery of the air was not brought about by daring alone. He was a cunning fighter and in a short space of time developed techniques which had devastating effects. One epic action epitomises his skill and courage. It took place early in 1917 when Ball, alone and hunting for action behind the enemy lines, spotted two German Albatros fighters scurrying back to their base after patrolling their own lines. Ball had the advantage of height and banked sharply, dropping the Nieuport's nose as he did so, and lunging towards the two Germans. He cocked his guns. The enemy had not spotted him but soon the roar of his engine reached their ears. Both pilots turned their heads in unison and saw the red-nosed craft plunge down towards them. Instantly they broke formation.

Ball selected his victim and closed for the kill, holding his fire until the last minute when he knew he would find the mark. The rattle of his guns shook the Scout. Bullets ripped and tore into the Albatros, shattering struts and puncturing the canvas. The German threw his aircraft about the sky but Ball was there behind him, as if glued to his tail. But the fatal blow eluded the British pilot. Bullets continued to tear into the German but still he remained airborne and in control. Then the worst happened. Ball's machine-guns fell silent. He had run out of ammunition.

By then the German plane was a tattered wreck but still flying. Realising what had happened and that his adversary had run out of ammunition, the German turned for home. The other Albatros, knowing that it was the legendary Ball with whom his companion was tangling was already on his way back to base. But Ball was not a man to give up easily. He stayed on the tail of the limping enemy plane and pulled out his .38 revolver. Steadying the Scout with his left hand on the joystick, he levelled the revolver at the German and fired six shots. But in the turbulent air and with the aircraft bucking and jinking in the currents, he missed. Ball was damned if he would give up and he followed the Albatroses back to their airfield deep behind enemy lines, only to watch in frustration as they both landed safely.

Anger, an unusual characteristic in Ball, got the better of him as he wheeled around above the German airfield. From the ground, riflemen took pot-shots at him but their aim was off. Ball determined that he would not be outdone, pulled a notepad from his flying suit pocket and scribbled a message on it. It was a challenge to the two Albatroses to do battle with him again at dawn the following day. Diving low over the airfield amid a hail of rifle shots, he dropped the note, then lifted the Scout's nose into the air in a climb, glancing back to watch a group of figures rushing to get the piece of paper. They had got the challenge. But would they take him up on it?

The following day, as the first light of dawn crept over Ball's airfield he climbed into the cockpit of the Nieuport Scout and strapped himself in. Soon the engine was breaking the stillness of the early morning and Ball was airborne on his way towards the German airfield. He skipped over the German lines until there before him lay the enemy's den and above it, two Albatroses. They had accepted the challenge.

Ball, always the believer in bold tactics, did not linger. Jabbing the throttle forward he bolted into the attack, picking the nearer of the two Germans as his target. 'First come first served,' he thought. With his finger curled round the trigger of his guns, his intent eyes never left the target as it loomed larger in his sights. He sensed that the German was nervous and would break away as the charging Nieuport closed in. He was an easy target – a sitting duck. It was all just too easy and Ball's mind suspected that all was not what it appeared to be. The German was taking no evasive action and he must by then have seen Ball coming. Before realisation dawned upon the British pilot, it was too late.

Suddenly a hail of bullets whipped past his aircraft from above. In an instant Ball broke off the attack and pulled hard back on the control column, ramming on more power as he did so. The Scout shot upwards. He had been lured into a trap. What a fool he had been, he thought, to fall for such an obvious ambush. There, above him, and plummeting down with guns blazing were three other Albatroses. His adversaries had brought along some chums in support. The age of chivalry had, it seemed, died. Ball was too great a prize to lose through any scruples of honour.

Ball was cornered; the odds were five to one against him getting out alive. To anyone other than the demonic Ball such odds would have meant death. But he kept cool. He turned on the Germans who were by now wheeling around him, closing in for a concerted kill. If he was to go, he would make damn sure he took some of them with him.

The Germans must have burned the midnight oil devising tactics to put paid to the British ace. While three of them lurked behind him, cutting off his line of retreat, the other two defiantly presented themselves as easy targets. Then, when Ball dashed in to get a burst at them, they bolted out of range, luring him farther into their own territory. These were cunningly devised tactics and deserved full marks for ingenuity. But they had reckoned without the cunning of the British master pilot. It soon became clear to him just what their game was. He fired burst after burst at all five aircraft as he gyrated about the sky but then the worst happened: his guns ran out of ammunition again. Now it seemed he was doomed. He was at their mercy. He knew it – and so did they. There could be only seconds left for him to live.

Now the two Germans he had been chasing turned on Ball to deliver the *coup de grâce*. Both of them bored in on him with guns chattering in a cone of bullets at the Scout and almost instantly the Nieuport fell away into a steep spin, tumbling out of control towards the ground. The three Albatroses which had watched the kill left the scene to return to their base, satisfied that the great British ace had finally met his end.

Ball's aircraft corkscrewed downwards with the two remaining German planes following it. They wanted to see the end of the man who had dared to challenge them to a duel. They watched intently as the Scout hurtled closer and closer to the ground. Then, with only a couple of hundred feet to spare, the Scout pulled up out of the spin and levelled off. Skipping over some trees, the British plane nosed towards a field, bumped down on to the ground, swerving crazily, then finally slewed to a halt.

The Germans watched fascinated, realising that Ball could only have been wounded. One German signalled to the other to land in the field. His intention was clear. He would capture the British pilot. They both touched down and taxied up close by Ball's Nieuport. As they leapt from their aircraft they could see Ball slumped forward in the cockpit with his engine still ticking over. Then they stopped dead in their tracks as the pilot suddenly came to life. His engine roared and they watched in dumb fury as the Scout darted across the grass and lifted into the air. They had been duped. Ball circled the field, waving to the two furious German pilots on the ground before heading back for his own base.

Ball's contradictory life continued. In the air he was a demon, on the ground, a quiet recluse, tending a small patch of flowers, playing his violin or tinkering with the engine of his aircraft. Throughout it all, his score shot up dramatically until he became the first British ace to receive public acclaim. By now a captain, Ball was ordered home for leave.

On his arrival in England he found himself headline news in all the papers. He was decorated with the Military Cross and subsequently admitted to the Distinguished Service Order. His daring in the air not only boosted the morale of his fellow countrymen but was an inspiration to the young pilots who followed in his wake.

Ball the national – but reluctant – hero was fêted and overwhelmed by the adulation of every Briton. This he found a greater ordeal than facing the Fokkers in the air over France. His shy nature rebelled against publicity. Britain needed a hero at that time when the war in the air was a desperate struggle and the war on the ground seemed to be going on for ever. Ball was their man and they resolved to preserve him, put him on show as the returning hero. He wanted none of it, but he had no choice. He was made a freeman of his native city of Nottingham and public appearances became daily events. Now he longed to be back in France, but the RFC had other plans for him. They could not risk losing such a hero and Ball was appointed to a pilot training school as an instructor in battle tactics. The job was safe, away from the horrors of France, but to Ball it was boring beyond belief and he pestered his commander at every opportunity to allow him to go back to France. For weeks he pleaded for a reprieve from the monotony of instructing and from exposure to the public, until at last permission was grudgingly granted.

As Ball flew his Nieuport across the French coast he saw a chance of letting the Germans know that he was back again. He sighted a large formation of enemy aircraft, enough to scare off the most courageous of British pilots – but not Albert Ball. Guns cocked, he was dashing in on them, plunging into the formation. In the opening seconds he shot down two of the German fighters. Then he prudently made himself scarce before the enemy could collect their wits and retaliate. Ball was back at war.

Within a couple of hours of his arrival at the British base he was airborne again, but Ball did not have things all his own way. Once, while flying alone over his favourite hunting ground, he saw twelve enemy fighters. Undeterred by the overwhelming odds against him, he launched his attack with typical dash, claiming three fighters before retreating. He would have remained amid the mêlée of enemy planes had he not run out of ammunition.

Ball bolted back to his base; without leaving his cockpit he replenished his supply of ammunition drums then turned tail and was off once more. Back he went to his favourite haunt but this time he found no fewer than fourteen of Germany's best fighters lying in wait for him. They had predicted his return and were out in strength to get him. Disregarding the danger, he sped in among them with savage determination, his guns blazing. But now the Germans held their stations. They wheeled round in circles, embracing him in an ever decreasing ring, determined to strangle the loner into submission and defeat. Ball had known all along that sooner or later his time would come and it seemed to him that this was it. The German aircraft played cat and mouse with him, leaping in, firing a burst of bullets then retreating. These pilots were no amateurs. Their bullets found their mark, shredding the canvas, shattering control lines, smashing the rear-view mirror, blasting away struts and worst of all, severing a fuel line. Instantly petrol poured out of the fractured line in a stream. One spark and he would become enveloped in flame. Ball knew that he was beaten and would have to get out quickly – or not at all.

His mastery of the Nieuport Scout saved him that day. Straining the crippled aircraft to its very limits, he squirmed clear of the enemy and sped for his own lines. By then his petrol tank had only a trickle of fuel left in it and it looked as if he would not make it into friendly territory. The trenches slid by beneath him, barely visible in the growing gloom of twilight. He could just make out a field ahead of him and he put the Scout down on it.

Ball's aeroplane was in a pitiful state. Indeed, she looked as if she would never fly again but Ball repaired the split fuel line, tied together the broken control lines and patched her up as best he could. Meanwhile darkness had overtaken him; he climbed into his cockpit and settled down to sleep. The following morning he awoke, took off and landed back at base.

One day Ball met his match . . . Again alone and flying over enemy territory, he sighted a German single-seater fighter. The reactions of both pilots were instantaneous. They turned on each other and a bitter fight began but try as both of them might, neither could gain the advantage of the other. They tried every trick in the book. Their courage and daring were equally matched. Their guns blazed and both inflicted slight damage on their opponent's aircraft but no more than a small chip out of a strut or the harmless perforation of a piece of canvas. The fight had reached an impasse and, when both of them ran out of ammunition, they realised that the fight could end in nothing other than a draw. Together they burst into peals of laughter and waved in mutual admiration before parting company and returning to their respective bases. Ball never did discover who his rival had been.

To this day, no one knows for certain how Albert Ball met his death. On 7 May 1917 he took off on patrol, this time in an SE5 fighter. He was soon in the midst of a furious dog-fight in which many aircraft were shot down. Ball's fighter was seen to disappear into cloud, then sometime later its wreckage was found near Annoeullin, not far from Lens, behind the German lines. Ball lay in the cockpit – dead.

Theories as to how he met his death abound. There are those who claim that he was shot down by Lothar von Richthofen, brother of the famous Red Baron but there is no truth in that theory. Others say that he was shot in the head by a German sharp-shooter hidden in the tower of a church at Annoeullin as he swept past in a low dive. There are also accounts of the incident that say he was completely overwhelmed by more than twenty German fighters and fell to their guns. Whatever the truth, of one thing there is absolutely no doubt, he died the way he fought – bravely and alone.

The Germans buried him with full military honours in the Cemetery of Honour at Annoeullin and carved a laurel leaf upon a cross which bore these words: 'He gave his life for his Fatherland.'

In a short, but spectacular career, Albert Ball had shot down forty-four enemy aircraft in more than one hundred and fifty air battles and played a significant part in changing the course of the war in the air. For this, Captain Albert Ball DSO and two Bars, MC, was posthumously awarded his country's highest decoration for valour, the Victoria Cross.

The fighter pilots of the day were almost to a man portrayed as fun-loving, gay cavaliers of the sky. Many of them were and most of these had good cause to cram their lives into a few short months or even less, for they knew they had not long to live. Many died in the opening rounds of their aerial battles. Yet the strange thing is that it was the odd-men-out who became the masters of the air, and surely none could have been a more unlikely candidate for aerial warfare than the tubercular young Frenchman, Georges Guynemer. But not only did he become a top-scoring fighter ace, he, like Ball, provided the Great War with one of its strangest mysteries.

Although the great breakthrough in powered flight had taken place in the United States of America, it was in France that the most significant strides were made in the early development of the aeroplane. The French had a mania for flying. The whole nation had caught the flying bug and none more than young Georges Guynemer, the son of a Paris lawyer. His love of aircraft reached obsessive proportions. He haunted airfields, going to any lengths just to get close to an aeroplane.

Like Ball, Guynemer was something of a recluse, living a hermit-like existence which had been forced upon him from childhood by having to spend long periods in sanatoria. He was so slim that his physical proportions resembled those of a girl rather than a boy. He suffered from chronic tuberculosis, a withering, crippling affliction which inevitably brought early death.

Guynemer's sole desire in life was to fly an aeroplane and he saw his chance to fulfil that dream when Europe erupted into war in 1914. But when he made approaches to the authorities about becoming a student pilot, the reaction was one of incredulous and almost cruel laughter. This fragile little youngster? It was *men* they wanted to fly their fighters, not their shadows. Indeed there was considerable doubt as to whether Guynemer would be suitable for military service at all.

As it was, Guynemer's insistence won him a job on the flying training field at Vauciennes, a little way outside Paris. It was not as a pilot, but as a 'broom basher', sweeping up and doing any odd job that needed doing. In almost constant pain from the tuberculosis that racked his chest, he never for a moment allowed that to dowse the fire of resolution that stoked his dream to become a pilot. At least for the time being he was near aeroplanes but their close proximity only served to heighten his passion. At every opportunity, Guynemer slipped into the workshops, eager to lend a hand. His enthusiasm was infectious and the mechanics were dumbfounded at his knowledge of aeroplanes. Word of this strange, but remarkable, young man spread and he came to the notice of the commander of the air base, who took a special interest in him.

Guynemer told the officer of his desire to become a pilot but kept secret the killer disease from which he suffered. Like Ball, he met with stiff opposition but persistence paid off and the young Frenchman was enlisted as a student pilot. Unlike Ball, Guynemer was a 'natural'. If there is such a thing as a born flier, Guynemer was it. He and the aeroplane were as one. He controlled the aircraft with superb ease, loving every second of the flight.

Guynemer had never known such joy at the thrill of flight. It more than lived up to his expectations. That first flight took place on 26 July 1915 and it was nothing short of dazzling. Other pilots who watched in awe from the ground refused to believe that young Guynemer had never flown before.

He qualified as a pilot in record time and astounded a whole nation by claiming his first kill in the very same month in which he had first flown. It was a fierce clash with a German Aviatik fighter, a superior machine to Guynemer's, but he won the day by sheer skill and sent the enemy machine tumbling to the ground. For this astounding feat, he was awarded the Médaille Militaire.

Guynemer had an astonishing temperamental resemblance to Albert Ball. On the ground no one would believe that this timid, pale-faced youngster was a fighter pilot, but in the air he was ruthless, daring and every bit the professional, a killer who knew that his time on this earth was limited and determined that, if he were to go, then he would go fighting.

His manifest courage and superb skill soon had his score mounting at an amazing rate but not all the missions he flew were in combat. He had a more sinister role to play when he swopped his single-seat fighter for a two seater . . .

Guynemer's passenger was an espionage agent, and the pilot's job was to get him behind the enemy lines to carry out acts of sabotage and spy upon the Germans. These excursions into enemy territory were hazardous pursuits. Guynemer had to skirt the concentrations of enemy troops and land his agent unseen, then return at a prearranged date and time to pick him up again. He claimed that these missions were far more frightening than the battles in the air. There was something devious and underhand about ferrying agents into enemy territory. He was much more at home in an open and clean dog-fight. Guynemer's favourite aircraft, the Nieuport and the Spad, which could reach a maximum speed of 130 miles an hour, were the scourge of the German Air Service. But invincible as Guynemer may have seemed, there was a flaw in his make-up. He was impulsive, and this characteristic was almost his undoing.

A new Nieuport arrived at the airfield and in one of his moments of impulse, Guynemer, having nothing better to do, took her aloft for a trial spin. The brand new aircraft was very much more powerful than any Guynemer had handled before and as he played about the sky with it, getting the feel of the new plane, he was 'jumped' by two German fighters. They darted in on him from behind and it was only at the very last moment that the Frenchman saw them on his tail. He rammed on full throttle and pulled hard back on the control column, rearing upwards in a vertical climb. As he soared upward, the German gunners opened up at his exposed fuselage and riddled it with bullets. The missiles smashed into the Nieuport's engine then into the cockpit where two of them thrashed into Guynemer's left arm.

The aircraft dropped from the sky and the Germans, thinking they had got their man, headed back home. Guynemer only just managed to level off using his right hand, his left arm hanging limp and useless by his side. Moments later, the Nieuport thudded into the ground a hair's breadth from the Allied trenches. Guynemer got out alive but badly wounded.

Caution, Guynemer felt, was the undoing of many a brave pilot. He had come close to death in that encounter with the German fighters but it did not alter his tactics. When his wounds had healed he was airborne again. His dare-devilry bore staggering fruit and by the end of 1916 his score had mounted to twenty-five enemy aircraft destroyed. Throughout the first nine months of the following year, he added another twenty-nine to that total, giving him fifty-four German kills to his credit, many of them in his favourite Spad aircraft which he had christened 'le vieux Charles'.

But while Guynemer's fame was in the ascendant, his health was deteriorating fast. The tuberculosis which had plagued him from birth was speeding up the fatal process, although he never allowed it to impair his skill in the air or let it be known to anyone save his few close comrades. Death he knew was close . . . but it was very much closer than he imagined.

On a foggy morning in September 1917, 'le vieux Charles' took to the air, followed by another fighter flown by one of Guynemer's close friends, Lieutenant Bozon-Verdurez. They were out for early morning prey – and they found it in the shape of a German fighter close by the front line.

Guynemer went in first with Bozon-Verdurez hugging his tail. Their intention was to attack the German from below and behind, his most vulnerable spot. Weaving so as not to give the German rear-gunner an easy shot, Guynemer opened up with his machine-guns, but his bursts of fire missed. Bozon-Verdurez, hot on his comrade's heels, got in a few bursts but these also missed. Both aircraft hurtled past the German and winged over to come in again for another attack but as they were doing so they caught sight of a swarm of German aircraft. Bozon-Verdurez signalled to Guynemer that he would make a bolt for it and act as a lure for the oncoming pack of Germans and he swept away. They saw him and bolted towards him. In the meanwhile, Guynemer turned his attention to the lone German, bent upon destroying him.

Bozon-Verdurez cast a backward glance and saw his friend going in for the attack. A few moments later, the German fighters were on to Bozon-Verdurez but the encounter was short and sharp. Their leader had clearly seen that the Frenchman was a lure and he took his squadron after Guynemer.

Seeing this, Bozon-Verdurez wheeled round to go to

Guynemer's aid – but Guynemer was gone. There was no sign of him. Only the German aircraft could be seen, homeward bound. Surely, the Frenchman thought, that lone German could not have shot down Guynemer. He searched the area, scouring the ground for a crashed aircraft but there was nothing, only the small village of Poelcappelle and around it a wide expanse of German-held country.

Finally Bozon-Verdurez had to give up the search. His fuel was running low and he headed back to the base, all the time hoping that he would see 'le vieux Charles'. But there was no sign of Guynemer.

When Bozon-Verdurez touched down at his airfield his worst fears were confirmed. Guynemer had not returned.

One by one aircraft took off from the field to go in search of the ace. None found any trace of him. Signals were sent out to the front in a desperate attempt to discover if anyone had seen a French fighter fall to the ground about the time of the fatal encounter. There were no witnesses.

So where was he? A prisoner of the Germans? No. Although the Germans did lay claim to having shot him down they made two glaring errors in the note they dropped on to a British airfield. It stated that 'Captain Guynemer was shot down and killed at 8 am on 10 September.' Their first mistake was the date. Guynemer disappeared on the 11th. But even if they had made a genuine error over the date they were quite wrong about the time, for at 8 am on the 11th, Guynemer was still having breakfast and did not take off with Bozon-Verdurez until at least half an hour later and the encounter with the German aircraft was some time after that.

Guynemer had, it seemed, vanished without trace. Every effort was made to solve the mystery of his disappearance. The little village of Poelcappelle subsequently fell into Allied hands and a thorough search was made of its graveyard and the area around it for fresh graves or the wreckage of Guynemer's Spad. Nothing was found.

When the news of the ace's disappearance was broken, rumours naturally ran rife. Wild stories abounded. Villagers in Poelcappelle told of how a Spad had crashed on its outskirts and three German soldiers had found it with a badly injured pilot still in the cockpit. But the spot at which the Spad was reputed to have crashed was unmarked. There was no sign of wreckage and even long after the war was over, none of the many people who set out to investigate the ace's disappearance could trace the three Germans who were supposed to have found him.

The German propaganda machine swung into action when their theory that their planes had shot him down was exploded by its glaring falsities. German newspapers proclaimed that Guynemer had died of tuberculosis, that the story of his mysterious disappearance was one of pure fabrication put out by the French to sustain Guynemer's heroic image. The German press even went to the extent of claiming that after Guynemer had died naturally of chronic tuberculosis, the French had strapped his body into the cockpit of his Spad and set the aircraft to take off and eventually crash, giving the impression that he had died an airman's death. How the French could possibly have achieved such a thing in those days is beyond comprehension.

The French preferred to believe that their legendary figure, Georges Guynemer, had flown so high that he could not come down again!

In the sixty years that have elapsed since Guynemer's disappearance, no one has been able to prove conclusively how he died. Unquestionably, however, he, like Ball, died the death that comes to those who fight alone, an exit from life shrouded in question and mystery.

There was no doubt about the fate of that other great ace, Edward 'Mick' Mannock, blind in one eye, who became the top-scoring fighter pilot in the Royal Flying Corps and subsequently the Royal Air Force.

To Mannock shooting down enemy aircraft was the means by which he could satisfy a bitter, obsessional hatred of the enemy. Not for him the sporting attitude of his fellow fighter pilots. He was no cavalier of the sky but a cold, calculating and utterly ruthless killer, merciless in his pursuit of the enemy.

Mick Mannock was a man of violence bent upon the annihilation of the entire German Army Air Service. He engaged himself in a one-man vendetta against the enemy. He was a brilliant leader and skilled tactician, admired and even idolised by his comrades, but certainly not liked. Mannock was, in effect, a hired killer and he took his job seriously, to the exclusion of all else. It was this, perhaps more than anything else, that made him a social outsider; a loner who, single-handed, evolved tactics which terrorised the Germans. But Mannock was himself a victim who had suffered a lifetime of persecution. As a child he had been surrounded by violence which was very often directed at him personally by a callous drunkard of a father who loathed the sight of his offspring. He was denied the love a normal child gets from his parents and, by a stroke of misfortune, the companionship of his contemporaries.

Mannock was born in the Cavalry Barracks of the Royal Scots Greys at Brighton in 1889, the son of a soldier in the Second Inniskilling Dragoons. Both his parents were Irish; his mother a quiet, reserved woman who was no match for the drunken bully she had married. Mannock senior did not care a fig for his wife or the family and spent the bulk of his soldier's pay on drink. Rolling in after a binge, he would invariably pick a fight with one of the family and more often than not it was Mick who bore the brunt of his father's temper. His loutish father settled arguments with his fists. Unsuccessful as a soldier and with little prospect of advancement, he gave vent to his frustrations by brutal assaults upon Mick, his other son, Patrick, and his two daughters. Under-fed and of slender build, the lanky Mick Mannock had a childhood of purgatory.

While still a child, Mick and his family travelled to India with their father who had been posted there. It was during his stay there that young Mannock contracted an illness which left him blind in his left eye, an affliction from which he was never to recover. The loss of sight in that eye had a profound effect upon Mannock. Children can often be incredibly, if innocently, cruel to others of their own age who are unfortunate enough to suffer some physical defect and Mick became the butt of their hurtful invective. Sensitive to the fact that he was not like other boys, he withdrew into a world of his own, shunning any communication with other children. His partial sight and frail physique made it difficult for him to join in games and he felt an outcast. To escape this humiliation as he saw it and the bitter reality of life in the turmoil of home, he took to wandering off into the country, alone with his thoughts. There he studied the abundant wild life and envied the animals and birds their freedom. One day, he resolved, he too would be free.

Mick's life continued along the same miserable course, punctuated only by brief periods of respite when his father was posted away and peace returned to the household. But these frequent departures of the family breadwinner left the Mannocks all but penniless. His mother brought the family back to England but, with no savings and only a pittance of an allowance from Mannock senior, the children went barefoot and ragged.

Necessity forced Mick to leave school at the age of thirteen to find work and help provide for the family's vital needs. Ill-equipped for anything other than labouring jobs and with a scarcity of employment, he had to take anything that came his way. His first employment was with a greengrocer, humping hundredweight sacks of potatoes from dawn till dusk. Often he returned home utterly exhausted with hands bleeding and blistered. All this for two shillings and sixpence a week.

He moved from job to job, improving his lot as he did so, but still not satisfied that he was achieving anything of great purpose. And above all, he wanted to make his mark, to compensate for the ills he had suffered in the past. A lucky break was at hand.

Mannock applied to be and was accepted as a clerk with the National Telephone Company. But he quickly found that sitting at a desk from nine till five was boring beyond belief. He wanted to get out and about into something more active, so he asked to be taken on as a telephone linesman. He was accepted and sent to Wellingborough in Northamptonshire to learn the tricks of the trade.

In Wellingborough he found himself lodgings in the house of Jim Eyles and his wife, both much older than Mannock but kind and homely folk who took an instant liking to the young man. Mannock reciprocated and a bond of friendship was struck which was to have a lasting effect upon him. He had found affection such as he had never had from his own family.

When he was offered the opportunity of taking up a job as a linesman in a remote region of Turkey the chance seemed too great to miss. With heavy heart he left the Eyles and travelled to Turkey. It was 1914. War was only a few months away and when it came, the Turks sided with the Germans. The result was arrest for Mannock and imprisonment in an internment camp for enemy aliens.

Mannock refused to countenance the prospect of rotting in that camp for the duration of the war and, for the first time in his life, his sight disability was to come to his aid. He proved to the authorities that because of his defective eye-sight, he must be regarded as a non-combatant and therefore could be of no service to his country in the prosecution of the war. It worked, and Mannock found himself en route back to England. When he got back to Wellingborough, he enlisted in the Army. To his dismay he was posted to the Royal Army Medical Corps: he did not relish the prospect of playing a passive role in the war. He wanted to be in the thick of the fighting so he applied for a transfer – and was posted to the Royal Engineers. But even this was not enough, despite the fact that he was commissioned. He quickly became disenchanted and looked around for something which might offer more excitement. He was to find it quite by chance when he met an old acquaintance who had joined the Royal Flying Corps and was undergoing pilot training. When he related some of his stories of flying, they immediately caught Mannock's imagination. He resolved then to apply for a transfer to the RFC but there was what appeared to be an insurmountable obstacle in his path. How could he ever hope to pass the stiff medical examination with only one good eye? His friend had a look at the eye and pointed out that it looked just the same as the other. In fact even he had been fooled. If Mannock could fool a friend, then why not the medical officer who was to examine him?

His application for a transfer to the RFC was granted and the day soon came when he had to go before the doctor. Before the appointed hour he crept into the empty surgery and memorised the letters on the eye chart then retreated. An hour or so later, his time came for the medical. It was thorough and he passed with flying colours but then came the eye test.

'Cover one eye with your hand and read the letters on this card,' the doctor ordered.

Mannock covered his left, blind eye and read the letters perfectly.

'And now the same again but cover the other eye this time,' the doctor said, turning to look at the chart and check Mannock's reading. Instead of covering his good eye, Mannock covered the blind one and read off the letters.

'Excellent,' the doctor pronounced. 'You've got a clean bill of health.'

Mannock's flying training was punctuated by a series of near disasters. Like Ball, he was no natural and with the added disability of blindness in one eye, his training was doubly difficult.

Judging distance was a particular problem and the ability to judge distance is a critical requirement for a pilot. In fact his flying was so bad that the commanding officer was on the point of rejecting him completely when a saviour arrived upon the scene in the form of Lieutenant James McCudden. McCudden was already an ace with a formidable score of kills to his credit and had been sent to England for a rest. Instead of resting he volunteered to pass on the wisdom of his experience as a pilot to trainee fliers. It was then that he met Mannock.

It did not take the ace long to detect Mannock's problem and discover that he was totally blind in his left eye. He spotted it at shooting practice after witnessing Mannock's abysmal performance. Mannock had no choice but to admit the defect.

McCudden would have been perfectly justified in 'shopping' Mannock which would have resulted in his being grounded permanently. But the ace admired the student's determination and took him under his wing, coaching him not only in the finer points of flying but also in aerial shooting. McCudden was a patient teacher and his airborne tutorials paid off. Using the tips given him by McCudden, Mannock soon became a crack shot and his flying improved to such an extent that in March 1917, he was awarded his wings. Now he itched to get into battle . . .

Mannock was posted to No 40 Squadron, one of the crack squadrons in the war zone, flying out of an airfield at St Omer in northern France. But he had no sooner arrived there than the old feeling of inferiority returned. He was very much the odd man out. He came of a humble background and, without the private income most of his fellow pilots had, he felt like a tramp among kings. The upshot of this was a retreat from the mess parties which were a frequent part of the fliers' lives in those days. He preferred his own company, away from the 'toffs', and any approach by them in the way of friendship was met by a rebuff. He was sullen and argumentative . . . and he had his own ideas about how the air war should be fought. His comrades took an instant dislike to the newcomer who, still 'wet behind the ears', was telling experienced fighter pilots how to win the war in the air.

It was two months before Mannock got his first kill and that was a German observation balloon which he could hardly have missed. His superiors were not impressed by his performance – or rather the lack of it. There were whispers that his behaviour in battle was little short of cowardly. He showed undue caution when engaging the enemy and earned himself the nick-name 'Windy' Mannock. The truth was that he was bewildered by the confusion of dog-fights when he became involved in them. He preferred to stalk his prey and attack from a position of advantage rather than get involved in the mêlée of a dog-fight where accurate shooting was extremely difficult. The tactics of the dog-fight were, he maintained, utterly wrong and he did not hesitate in airing his views on the subject. For someone who had not a single enemy aircraft to his credit, he was treading on shaky ground. The cocky confidence he showed in his theories only served to encourage hostility towards him in the mess but he continued to argue vehemently that he was right. Outwardly, he gave the impression of not caring a damn what his fellows thought of him but in reality the hostile looks and the sneering hurt him deeply, though he would never admit it. Mannock knew that acceptance would only be gained by proving that his theories were right . . .

He spent every free moment studying tactics employed both by the Allies and the Germans, searching out their strong points and their weaknesses. From this he developed a technique which was to shake the German Air Service. His golden rule was to attack in strength, never alone as Albert Ball had. He became the fox and the Germans the chickens and he dealt with them with the same cunning, stealth and ferocity. It paid dividends and in the first nine months of his tour he blasted six German aircraft out of the sky, earning himself the accolade of an 'ace', a Military Cross and Bar, but most of all the respect, if not the friendship, of his fellow fighter-pilots.

Mannock perfected the technique of deflection shooting: instead of taking the easy course of flying behind his opponent and shooting him down from there, he chose the more difficult shot and dashed in on the enemy's flank to rake the entire length of the machine with fire.

'Aim for the pilot. He's the bastard you want to destroy. Kill him and you've got the plane as well,' he would preach. 'No point in winging the aeroplane. If he lands safely, the plane can be patched up and he can fly again. No use wounding him. You want him *dead*!'

However murderous Mannock's approach to war might have

been, he was of course right. It was one thing destroying an enemy plane. It could be replaced by another off the assembly line. It was quite a different proposition training a fledgeling pilot and moulding him into a fighter. Indeed, partly as a result of Mannock's tactics, the German Air Service lost many of its best pilots and were losing the battle because they had to use youngsters untried in battle.

Such was Mannock's success that he was promoted to flight commander and this gave him fresh opportunities for launching attacks using his own techniques. He became a leader without peer, utterly professional and painstaking in the perfection of his own performance and that of his pilots. After every mission, he would carry out a searching autopsy, examining every move that had been made, pointing out to his pilots where they had gone wrong or where some manoeuvre needed improving.

Mannock had no time for the demonstrative pilot, the daredevil. There was no room for heroics in his scheme and he could be ruthless with anyone who did not follow his instructions to the letter. Fancy flying was not for him – or his pilots. It is said that on one occasion he actually shot over the top of one of his own aircraft, loosing off a dozen or so rounds over the head of a pilot in his flight when he committed some small misdemeanour on a mission!

As Mannock's war progressed so too did his hatred of the enemy, particularly when Mannock had to pass through areas which had been shelled or where battles had recently taken place. There he saw at first hand the real horror of war and the enormous slaughter in which it resulted.

Once when he had shot down a German two-seater he watched it crash-land in a field. He realised that the pilot and observer were still alive so he dived down on the defenceless, wrecked aircraft and set about spraying it with machine-gun fire until its crew lay motionless and dead. He was heartless in the pursuit of his prey.

Mannock's attitude is perhaps best illustrated by an incident which occurred one day in 1918 when he returned to the squadron mess to hear that the great German ace, Baron Manfred von Richthofen, had been killed. When someone proposed a toast to the memory of the enemy ace, Mannock marched resolutely out of the mess, mouthing oaths as he went. His sole regret was that it had not been *he* who had shot down Richthofen.

In spite of this hard exterior, Mannock had his own inner fears. He had witnessed large numbers of British and German aircraft plunging to the ground in flames and he knew that, one day, such a fate might befall him too. His dreams were tortured by this thought and night after night he would waken drenched in sweat having seen himself tumble to the ground in a burning aircraft from which there was no escape. As time went on this fear grew, but never for a moment did he falter in pressing home his attacks.

Mannock's score of victories soon topped fifty and he was admitted to the Distinguished Service Order, but medals meant nothing to him even when, a short time later, he was awarded a Bar to his DSO. The only importance medals had for Mannock was that they signified a greater number of kills.

The pace at which Mannock fought was exhausting. He flew almost every day, dicing with death all the time and the tension of the fray made a deep impression upon him. Others noticed this and eventually he was sent home to England with strict instructions to take a rest. Reluctantly he left, but not before having a final fling against the enemy only an hour before his departure.

Mannock's 'breather' between rounds in the fight was brief and when he returned to France, he was promoted to the rank of Major and given his own squadron. But his elation was cut short when the news reached him that his friend and former tutor, James McCudden, had been killed while taking off on a mission. Mannock, never one to show emotion, wept.

He resolved that his friend's death must be avenged. His score of kills rocketed into the sixties and he delighted in the thought that each victory in the sky was another toll exacted for McCudden.

Soon his score entered the seventies and he caught up with the reigning champion ace, Major 'Billy' Bishop, whose tally was then seventy-two. It now became something of an obsession with Mannock that he should get another kill to become the supreme ace of aces in the Allied camp. But it was about this time that he got his strongest ever premonition of death, one that he could not hide from his closest colleagues. He confessed to Taffy Jones, a flight commander: 'I'm just like any other pilot. I'm scared stiff when I see my Hun floating down in flames.'

Jones could see that Mannock was deeply depressed and he

made an effort to wrest his commander from it but just then they were joined by one of the new boys of the squadron, Lieutenant Inglis, a New Zealander who had yet to score a kill against the enemy. As if trying to snap himself out of his gloom, Mannock turned to Inglis and said: 'Have you got yourself a Hun yet, Kiwi?'

'No, sir,' Inglis replied in a quiet voice, almost too afraid to admit it.

'Then come on, lad,' Mannock said rising from his seat. 'We'd better see what we can do about that, eh?'

Inglis followed Mannock out to the aircraft park. Mannock was the first into his cockpit with his engine revving into life but Inglis found he had elevator trouble and could not take off. Not noticing this, Mannock was airborne before he realised that he was alone. He pressed on into enemy territory but found no fodder for his guns and returned to base.

Inglis was disappointed but Mannock quickly reassured him by offering to take him hunting at dawn the following morning.

'We'll catch ourselves some early birds, eh?' he said confidently. 'But make sure your aircraft is serviceable!'

With that, Mannock returned to the mess and found Taffy. The glum expression returned to his face.

'I don't think I'm going to last much longer, Taffy,' he admitted. 'You watch yourself. Don't go following any Huns too low or you'll end up joining the "sizzle brigade" like me.'

The following morning Mannock waited for Inglis in a deserted mess. His mind was troubled; he had had a sleepless night, haunted by the spectre of his own demise. Finally Inglis arrived.

'Come on, Kiwi,' he said. 'We'll get up there and see if we can find a nice two-seater for you to bang away at.'

As they made their way out to the waiting aircraft, Mannock gave Inglis his final instructions.

'Now don't forget – keep close to my tail and follow my movements. If you're too far behind I'll waggle my wings. Okay?'

When he arrived at his aircraft, he did something he had never done before. He shook hands with all his mechanics as if in farewell. Then, as he climbed into his cockpit, one of them wished him success in getting his seventy-third Hun. The two aircraft roared, took off, and were soon gone from sight.

Inglis hugged Mannock's tail as he had been instructed, putting on little bursts of speed when his leader rocked his wings. Then, not far into enemy territory, Mannock banked sharply with his guns blazing. For a moment, Inglis wondered what was happening – then he saw it: right in front of them was a plump LVG German aircraft already riddled with holes from Mannock's guns. Inglis steadied his aircraft then fired a long burst which sent the aircraft tumbling earthwards with flames licking out of it.

Mannock, having achieved his seventy-third victory, followed the German down, breaking the rule he had expounded to Taffy the day before. As he fell lower, he flew rings around the burning German aircraft which spun downwards like a flaming torch. It was then that Inglis, watching the action from high above, saw Mannock's aircraft quite suddenly go out of control and lapse into a right-hand bank. Inglis watched amazed until he saw the faint flicker of flame lick out of the right-hand side of the aircraft. The tongues of flame spread rapidly over Mannock's plane until soon it was a raging furnace screeching towards the ground. Seconds later it exploded in a vast ball of fire.

Inglis was not to know it then but the Major's aircraft had been hit by machine-gun fire from the ground. The ace of aces was dead.

Stunned by what he had seen, Inglis swept low over the burning wreckage in which Mannock's charred body lay. He knew no one could have survived that crash and turned to head for home. No sooner had he done so than he too was hit by ground fire but he succeeded in limping back over the lines and landed in a field where British soldiers raced over to him. They found him sitting in his cockpit, sobbing and muttering over and over again, the same words: 'They've shot down my major . . .'

In spite of an intensive search, no trace was ever found of Mannock's machine or his body. His adopted father, Jim Eyles, continued the search well after the war was over but found nothing.

Major Edward 'Mick' Mannock DSO and Bar, MC and Bar, the most successful fighter pilot Britain has ever had, died in the way he feared most of all . . . in flames.

The ace with one eye, the loner and outcast had shown himself supreme in the air, unbeaten by any other airman. He was posthumously awarded the Victoria Cross. The citation read:

For bravery of the highest order ... This highly distinguished officer, during the whole of his career in the Royal Air Force, was an outstanding example of fearless courage, remarkable skill, devotion to duty and self sacrifice, which has never been surpassed.

Mannock had been 'accepted'.

3

The Melting of Johnny Snow

Preface

The world of espionage is one of duplicity, lies, half-truths, cover stories, code-names, double identities, forgery and, above all, secrecy. All these factors make a full account of a spy's activities almost impossible. The task of the author in writing the story of an agent's dealings is made all the more difficult if the spy in question was working for two masters. Spies are, occasionally by nature and certainly by training, accomplished liars, most especially when they are double agents. Even the spy-masters, those who dictate the deeds of their agents in the field, are unreliable sources of truth for, upon the cessation of hostilities, they are often reluctant to reveal in detail what they and their agents were about during the war, the reason being that they may have 'dirtied their hands' in their dealings and retribution may ensue.

The writer must therefore take what proven facts are available and link them together to weave a readable narrative. Since the end of the Second World War, mountains of books have been written on the subject of spies and spying, and although they purport to relate fact many are riddled with blatant inaccuracies and pure invention on the part of the writer.

In the course of my research for the chapter which follows, I referred to many sources as well as books written by authors of considerable repute. I found many of them to be at variance with each other. I have substantiated much of the evidence – but not all of it. It is for this reason that I have to make clear that, while the story is in essence true, I have taken the liberty of filling in certain gaps with events which *almost certainly* took place but which cannot be proved. For that same reason, I have chosen to identify some of the leading characters in the story by code-names or names of my own invention. Johnny Snow was a real person; his name is fictitious.

Johnny Snow was small in stature, but what he lacked in physique was more than compensated for by a voracious appetite for enormous excesses in everything he did. He was a womaniser who indulged himself in Casanovian intrigues not simply to satisfy an uncommonly strong sexual desire but to feed an ego infinitely greater than his frame could contain. He revelled in the company of attractive women with one 'affair' whetting his appetite for another. He drank the finest brands of Scotch whisky. He was rapacious and unscrupulous, both in his private and business lives, not unusual failings, and today Snow might well have gone unnoticed. But he reached the zenith of his bacchanalian and sexual binges in the 1930s when society was far less tolerant than it is now. His orgy of love-making and drinking came when the world was wresting itself from the abyss of a depression. It was a time of incredible hardship, of dole queues, soup kitchens, mass unemployment and desperate men struggling to feed their families on scraps. None of this touched Johnny Snow. His lust was boundless. But women, drink and high-living cost money and, although modestly successful in business, Snow – a married man with a family – could not pay the price to satisfy his insatiable desires. So he had to look around for some willing philanthropist who would supplement his income and subsidise his adventures. Finding such a pot of gold would be difficult in Britain, but he knew the world. He had travelled extensively and he mentally scanned its length and breadth, seeking out a likely 'bank' from which to find the funds.

Nazi Germany was in the ascendant, rising like a phoenix from the terrible years of the Weimar Republic under the leadership of Adolf Hitler. Johnny Snow had been there and seen that things were happening at a fast pace. There were rewards to get in such a country for the right person, someone willing to help it on its rise to power. Snow was sufficiently astute to recognise this.

'Johnny Snow' was not in fact 'born' until the 1930s, although he had been alive and well and living it up in the fleshpots of

Canada and Europe for some time before. He first drew breath in Wales in 1899 and grew up to become a fanatical Welsh Nationalist with a deep-seated hatred for England and everything English. A fluent Welsh speaker, he dreamt of the day when Wales would be free of the English yoke.

Snow went to Canada but returned to Britain in 1933 where his expertise in electronics came to the attention of an industrialist. He had developed an advanced form of accumulator in which the Royal Navy expressed a keen interest. The industrialist, sensing an inventive and lucrative property in Johnny Snow, took him into his company. He proved so good at his job that his patron financed the setting up of Snow's own electrical engineering company which acquired valuable Admiralty contracts, but not valuable enough for the Welshman.

Snow travelled extensively throughout Europe selling his wares and in doing so established many useful contacts. In the course of these business-cum-pleasure excursions he picked up tit-bits of information on foreign advances in his field and these he passed on to the Admiralty. The knowledge Snow passed on percolated through the Naval system and via Naval Intelligence to the British Secret Intelligence Service which was not slow to appreciate that Snow might be a source of even more important information. When a colonel in the SIS approached Snow and proposed that he should become a paid agent, he reacted with typical greed. For the moment at least, his Welsh patriotism was put aside in favour of what he imagined would be a rich source of income.

For a while, he brought back what intelligence he could glean from his visits to the Continent and in return was paid small but regular amounts of money. In time he found these sums insufficient and he insisted upon more, but the funds were not forthcoming.

Snow was a man who would sell his very soul to the devil – and he did. He saw a way of milking the British Secret Intelligence Service on the one hand and getting the cream from its potential adversary, the German Abwehr, Hitler's Secret Service. He could be of immense value to the Germans. With his military contracts he had virtual *carte blanche* to enter some of the country's most secret sites. Furthermore, he had allies in the Welsh National Party who held key posts at similar establishments. He could rely upon these friends, for their dislike of the

English was deep and was not founded upon monetary gain. Snow saw that he could build up a formidable spy-ring which, under his leadership, would not only prove lucrative for him but help in bringing down the nation he had grown to hate. But to achieve such an aim demanded cunning and caution. Snow had years of devious dealing behind him, some of it taught him by the SIS themselves and he meant to put it to good use.

First he had to make contact with the Abwehr and do so without the knowledge of the SIS. Snow lived in London's Hampstead district and knew the metropolis well. There were tight-knit communities of every nationality in London; foreigners who had come from their native lands to set up business in the great sprawling city. Some had been settled in the city for many years, others were comparative newcomers, but most had one thing in common, they kept in contact with each other, setting up clubs where they could meet and talk their own language as well as perpetuate their own customs. These social clubs were outwardly harmless meeting places but some, in particular the German Social Labour Club in Bayswater, was a 'front' for the Abwehr's espionage activities on Britain. Its manager, Herr Brunner, cast his net wide to catch anyone who might be useful to his masters in Germany.

Johnny Snow's attraction to the club in Cleveland Terrace was two-fold. It was handsomely endowed with nubile Fräuleins, exiled young beauties who eagerly sought company, particularly that of British visitors to the club. They were the bait, manipulated by Brunner to lure his customers as a pimp rules his prostitutes. Snow was quick to catch on to the set-up when he first visited the club and nothing could have satisfied him more. Soon he and Brunner were firm friends and, in the course of conversation, the talk turned to Snow's frequent visits to Europe. Neither man laid his cards on the table but each could read the other's mind. There was no talk of espionage. Snow did not reveal his willingness to work for the Germans nor did Brunner admit to being an Abwehr agent. Both knew without saying so.

The Welshman complained of how lonely his business trips to Europe were and how much he craved company in the evenings. Brunner got the point and he acted swiftly. On a subsequent visit to the club, Brunner took Snow's arm and led him aside from the crowded bar. An impish glint lit the German's eyes.

'I think I have found the answer to those lonely nights, Herr

Snow,' he said. 'Of course I have many friends in Germany but also some who travel as you do in the other countries of Europe. They are salesmen and engineers like yourself. They too get lonely and would like some company. Some are in your line of business. Who knows, perhaps you could put some business their way.'

Snow realised that already Brunner had been in contact with the Abwehr. Arrangements were being made. They were working fast. Snow had let slip enough about his business activities to excite the interest of the Germans and, if he was all he said he was, then here was a friendship worth cultivating. But the Abwehr was cautious. Snow could be a British 'plant' working for the SIS and out to penetrate the spy ring that Brunner and his masters had carefully set up in Britain. He would have to pass a rigorous test before being admitted to the ranks of the German Secret Service.

Brunner handed Snow a piece of paper. On it was written the name Konrad Pieper and a telephone number in Brussels. Pieper, Brunner explained, was in the electrical business and was a regular visitor to Brussels. He too was anxious to have company on his visits to the Belgian capital.

Snow left the club early that night. He had preparations to make. He had no visit to Brussels planned but he would quickly make sure that such a trip was arranged. Within a few days everything was prepared. When he arrived in Brussels he booked into the best hotel, secure in the knowledge that Herr Pieper was no electrical engineer but a vetting agent for the Abwehr.

Snow picked up the phone in his plush hotel room and rang the number Brunner had given him. Sure enough, Herr Pieper was due to arrive in Brussels the following day and would be very pleased to meet Herr Snow. By sheer coincidence, Herr Pieper too would be staying at the same hotel.

Konrad Pieper checked in to the hotel the next day and quickly made the acquaintance of the Welshman. Snow's conversations with Pieper were curiously one-sided, with the German soliciting information, asking short questions and leaving Snow to do most of the talking. Snow had half expected this. He was 'on trial' and he did well, letting slip tasty tit-bits to whet the appetite of the inquisitor.

Snow's meeting with Pieper was short. The German had got what he wanted and was satisfied that the Welshman could safely go on to the next stage in the proving course.

Snow returned to England a happy man and, a few days later, a letter arrived from an import-export company in Hamburg, Reinhold GMBH, offering to do business and inviting Snow to come to Hamburg for a meeting.

Snow sailed for Hamburg where he was made the guest of the Abwehr in the city's most luxurious hotel, the Vier Jahreszeiten, which overlooked the city's famous Alster lake. Such treatment was a mark of the Abwehr's undoubtedly vast financial resources and it greatly impressed the prospective spy. But there was another reason for Snow's delight at being in Hamburg: the notorious Reeperbahn, the mecca for the sexual deviant where every conceivable kind of sexual pleasure could be catered for. The Abwehr had chosen their meeting place with great care.

When they came face to face, Snow and the German he had come to meet knew that the time for a cover-up was over. Captain Dierks, a leading officer in the Abwehr, quickly established his true identity, admitting to Snow who he really was and Snow for his part revealed his willingness to work for the Abwehr. They shook hands to clinch the agreement, then relaxed to enjoy the multitudinous pleasures Hamburg offered.

Snow was in buoyant mood. Now he could enjoy his pleasures to the full. Now he would show the bloody English. Dierks entered into the spirit of the evening but behind the façade of outward merriment, he had niggling doubts about Snow. The German was by nature and training a cautious man. He trusted no one, least of all a pleasure-seeking Welshman who appeared over-eager to help the Reich. Snow's motivations were anti-English, or so he said, but during the course of that evening it became obvious to Dierks that here was a man whose sole aim in life was enjoyment. Such a man was not to be entirely trusted and Dierks vowed that, although he had accepted him, Snow would have to be closely watched.

Snow was completely unaware of Dierks's doubts. As far as he was concerned everything had gone off smoothly. This was apparently confirmed some days later when he was introduced to Captain Nikolaus Ritter, alias Dr Reinhold, alias Dr Rantzau, who was to be his contact and to whom he would impart the intelligence he collected in England.

Ritter, an astute and highly-trained member of Admiral Canaris's Abwehr staff briefed Snow on the sort of information he wanted. He knew of Snow's access to military establishments, notably Admiralty dockyards, and would welcome anything that his agent could pick up. He wanted to know everything, however unimportant it might seem to Snow. There was no hesitation on Snow's part, but Ritter, like Dierks, was initially wary.

In the two years that followed, Snow proved himself beyond the Abwehr's wildest expectations. He was richly rewarded for his efforts, receiving sums in excess of £2,000 each year, which in those days was a substantial amount. In the meantime, he continued to feed the Secret Intelligence Service with small scraps of information.

So the dynamic little Welshman carried on his legitimate business as an electrical engineer while also acting as a double agent. To the SIS he was known by the code-name 'Snow' and to the Abwehr by the code-name 'Johnny'. Hence the choice of the fictitious cover name 'Johnny Snow'. He served both his masters well but unquestionably his loyalty lay with the Germans.

Later, in 1939, he was hailed by Admiral Canaris himself as 'Johnny, the master spy'. The Chief of German Intelligence had good reason to dub Snow with such an accolade. He had given him information not only on naval projects but also secret information on work going on at the Royal Aircraft Experimental Establishment at Farnborough as well as at civilian contractors. He even reported the positions of airfields throughout the south of England, a piece of information that was to prove invaluable to Luftwaffe pilots when they began the Blitz of England in 1940.

But while Snow continued to delight his German masters, he had incurred the displeasure of the Secret Intelligence Service. His contempt for the English had been discerned by a particular colonel in the SIS. Apparently for this reason alone, the SIS kept a watch on him, tailing him for some time in England. Snow did nothing suspicious, until a letter came into the possession of the SIS. It was a letter from Snow to an address in Hamburg, an address which the SIS knew was a mailing box for the Abwehr. There could be little doubt that Snow was in touch with the German Secret Service. On his next trip to Europe, a tail was put on him and the Special Branch detective who followed Snow was led to a meeting between the Welshman and Ritter. The encounter was damning. The detective immediately headed back to England and informed the SIS, who lay in wait for the unsuspecting Snow when he arrived back in London.

Snow hardly had time to unpack his cases when the fateful knock on the door came and he was confronted by two Special Branch men, 'inviting' him to accompany them to SIS head-quarters. He was led to a car outside his house and was squeezed in between the two detectives in the back seat. No one said a word during the journey but Snow's brain was working at double speed. He had foreseen that such a thing might happen and had already concocted a cover story, so he was at least partially ready. Now, as the car sped along the London streets, he mentally put the final touches to the story.

The evidence against him was put straight to him when he met the colonel. There was a pause before he answered, then he drew a breath and began his explanation to the colonel and the cluster of SIS men who crowded the room. Far from attempting to wriggle out of it, he 'confessed' to his duplicity. His inquisitors were taken aback. There was no hesitation in his admission that he was an Abwehr agent but it was his explanation as to how he became a German spy that really left the SIS colonel open-mouthed.

Snow claimed that he had made contact with Pieper to get inside information for the British and that he had had to pay for it. He even went as far as saying that as a patriotic Briton, he had dipped into his own pocket to keep Pieper sweet. But Pieper's demands were too great for his pocket to sustain. When he told Pieper this, the German suggested that he join forces with the Abwehr and here he had seen an opportunity of pene-trating the German intelligence service. Pieper had arranged everything and the meeting he had just seen to in Europe was to enrol him as an Abwehr agent.

'I did it for Britain,' he said. Had he left the story without that additional plea, the colonel might conceivably have believed him, but he knew Snow too well.

'You don't seriously expect me to believe your story, do you?' he asked bluntly. 'The whole thing is a tissue of lies. You're a traitor. You joined up with the Abwehr for your own treacherous ideals and to line your own pockets. You're despicable, Snow! The most miserable, cringing little cretin it's ever been my displeasure to encounter. You're a traitor not just to England but to your native Wales as well and I'm going to see that you get your just deserts.'

The colonel, by now red-faced with anger, looked to the Special Branch men who had brought Snow to him.

'Take him out of my sight before I vomit. Charge him with . . .'

But the colonel did not get a chance to finish his sentence. Snow interrupted: 'I don't think you'll be charging me with anything, colonel,' Snow interjected with challenging lilt to his Welsh accent. His tone was threatening.

'If you put me on the stand in court I'll blow the gaff on everything including my connection with the Secret Service and that could be embarrassing for you, couldn't it?'

Snow was right, and the colonel knew it. The SIS had no alternative but to let him go. They could have had Snow 'eliminated' but, despite his anger, the colonel could see that there might be a use for Snow sometime in the future. It was safer to keep him within the ranks of the SIS, where he could be watched, rather than reject him.

'Very well', the colonel conceded. 'It appears that you've got me over a barrel. You'll be kept on with us but I warn you now, Snow, if there's the slightest suspicion that you're feeding the Abwehr with information which could hurt this country, you'll be dealt with and I mean properly.'

Snow had remained outwardly composed and almost cocky but he was badly shaken and realised that he would have to come up with something big by way of military intelligence from Germany to convince the SIS that he was firmly on their side. This he did, making frequent visits to Europe. No longer was he followed and he resumed his contacts with Ritter with whom he was developing a close personal friendship.

Snow's favourite haunt was the Valhalla Cabaret in the Reeperbahn. There was a system of telephone communications between each of the tables by which a man, or a woman for that matter, could call someone at another table and invite them over. The purpose of the invitation was clear: a few drinks then bed. To Snow, this system of conquest was a mechanical marvel. Never had the telephone been put to better use. Surely, he mused, this was why it had been invented! He was like a child with a new toy and Ritter ensured that he was rarely rejected by the woman he called.

Snow's fascination for the female of the species did however have its dangers. He was, like most of his fellow countrymen, handsomely endowed with the gift of story-telling. Unfortunately, his stories flowed perilously close to the truth on a few occasions when he was the worse for drink and the company of some Aryan blondes. A boaster without peer he would tell tales to excite his female companions. What he did not realise was that some of his female friends and bed partners were Abwehr agents who warned their superiors of Snow's propensity towards story-telling. He was politely but firmly told to keep his mouth shut. From then on, his womanising was monitored by Ritter who 'selected' Snow's females for him. They were all completely trustworthy and Ritter knew that anything Snow might let slip would go no further.

Until the 1938 Munich crisis there had not been any great urgency about Johnny Snow's espionage but, with the imminent possibility of war between Britain and Germany, the situation changed dramatically. Canaris directed his subordinates to prepare for war by making provisions for the likelihood that agents like Snow would find themselves cut off in their own countries and unable to bring their information to Germany. The answer to the problem lay in radio communication and, in the early months of 1939, Snow went on a short but intense training course at the Abwehr's radio school outside Hamburg. He took along with him a new female acquisition, a mistress he had found in Britain.

Snow's behaviour at home had reached such an intolerable level that he and his wife had separated. He moved house to a suburb of London where he set up a cosy little nest with his new girl friend. He had walked the dangerous tight-rope of adulterous affairs which left his personal life in a tangled mess. Nevertheless, his spying was kept quite apart from sexual pursuits. It took considerable skill on his part to run three separate lives without their paths crossing. His organisational ability was quite exceptional and the more deeply involved he became in this knitted web of intrigue the better he liked it.

Arriving back in England complete with radio transmitter, he set to work to try it out, transmitting weather reports to the German Intelligence headquarters. Such information in time of war would, he knew, be of great value to an attacking air force and to the German navy. When his coded morse messages darted through the ether and reached the Germans they were delighted. Their investment was paying off with fat dividends and there were even greater things to come. Throughout 1939 and until war finally engulfed Europe, Snow continued to transmit between visits to Germany, and the content of his messages grew better as they progressed. He became increasingly adept in the use of his new toy and revelled in the congratulations which were showered on him by Ritter when he met up with him in Germany. He had, it seemed, pulled off a considerable coup – or so he thought.

Snow knew that the British had radio monitoring departments which kept a close watch on transmissions. The object was to detect illegal radio signals, trace them and discover just what was being sent. At considerable risk, Snow had carried out many transmissions and it appeared that none of them had been intercepted, for there had been no more knocks at the door, no swoops by the Special Branch. While this was initially something of a relief, Snow did become worried. He knew just how efficient the monitoring was and it struck him as odd that he had not been detected. Surely, he thought, the British must have picked up some of his transmissions. And if they had, then why had they not pounced. Were they playing cat and mouse with him?

As the weeks and months passed, he became increasingly nervous at the lack of British interest in his secret radio transmissions. There was one stark reality which Snow had to face and that was the possibility that the British had in fact detected the signals and were listening in but biding their time before swooping in to catch him, allowing him to incriminate himself beyond the point from which he could extricate himself.

Snow's skin was more precious than his relations with the Germans; he was no martyr. He therefore evolved a plan which he hoped would get him off the British hook and at the same time allow him to continue his profitable association with the Germans. For the second time in his career as a spy, he decided to 'come clean' and tell all.

Snow would make a present of his radio set to the SIS! It was a bold, but calculated move on Snow's part. He knew he would be giving the SIS something they had long sought, a German radio transmitter, together with the opportunity for foxing the enemy.

Before taking the plunge, however, Snow determined to impart to the Germans some vital information which had come his way via one of his contacts. Of all the information that he filtered through to the Germans, this little gem was the most precious. With the help of his friend, Snow had pinpointed the towering masts of a chain of radar stations which punctuated the south coast of England. With this radar the RAF would be able to determine the movements of the Luftwaffe across the Channel and be forewarned of impending attacks. It would enable the Royal Air Force to track German fighters and bombers and intercept them before they reached their targets. It was an extremely potent piece of scientific equipment and was destined to play a large part in determining the outcome of the Battle of Britain. Snow sent the information. His morse key tapped out the signal of doom that would eventually bring bombs raining down on these outposts, cripple the radar network and allow German bombers to unleash a terrible onslaught not only against the fighter stations but also the civilian population.

Ritter's joy at receiving Snow's revealing message was ecstatic. It confirmed the existence of radar. The Germans had heard of it but had had no positive and conclusive proof that it existed. Now they knew, thanks to their master spy.

Before Snow could make his gift to the SIS, Britain was at war with Germany, following the German invasion of Poland. The Abwehr, already on a war footing, rubbed its hands in glee at the prospect of great things from its master spy. The SIS too went on a war footing, closing its ranks for the fray and putting its house in order. Part of the clean-up concerned Johnny Snow.

Snow lifted the telephone receiver and dialled New Scotland Yard. In moments he was put through to the Special Branch and to an inspector there. He identified himself then went on: 'I have something which I am sure will be of interest to you.'

'I too have something for you,' the voice at the other end of the phone said in a tone which Snow could not identify.

'Good,' Johnny said and arranged to meet the detective that night at one of London's railway stations.

At the appointed time, Snow arrived at the station carrying a large suitcase. Inside the case was the radio transmitter/receiver. He recognised the inspector as he approached, accompanied by a colleague, and smiled in greeting. Both of the officers however remained stony faced.

'Well then, you're here,' Johnny began by way of opening the conversation. 'Good. Then we can get on with it,' he said, conscious that something was amiss.

'Yes, Snow, now we can get on with it, as you say,' the inspector agreed. 'If you'd like to come down to the Yard with us we can sort things out there.'

'Eh, yes, well,' Johnny began, a little surprised at the invitation. 'Do we, I mean, is there really any need for that?'

'Yes, Snow,' the inspector answered with a glance that confirmed Snow's fears that all was not well. 'A busy railway station is no place to conduct business, is it?'

Snow agreed and followed the two men to their car, which was parked outside the station. They got in and drove off. They had not gone far when Snow, nervous by now, posed the question: 'You said you had something for me,' Snow ventured tentatively, leaning forward towards the inspector in the front seat.

'Ah yes,' the detective said turning and taking a sheet of paper out of his breast pocket and handing it to Snow. 'I do indeed have something for you – a warrant for your arrest.'

Snow took the paper, his mouth half open in surprise.

'A warrant? You mean I'm under arrest? But what for?'

'Read the paper and you'll know' the inspector said tersely.

Snow unfolded the sheet of paper and read it as best he could in the dim light. Most of it was indecipherable but the pertinent words 'acts of espionage, prejudicial to . . .' were clear enough.

'This is ridiculous!' he protested. 'I'm as loyal as the next man and the SIS knows it. I work for them. I'm one of their best men,' he boasted. 'You speak to the colonel. He'll tell you.'

Snow's protestations were to no avail and the car swept into New Scotland Yard, its tall, round towers flanking and dominating the gateway. Snow was led out and into a room where he was confronted by the colonel from the SIS. He still carried the suitcase with its trump card inside.

'Well now, Snow,' the colonel began, smiling and revelling with delight that he was now in a position to crucify 'one of his best men'. 'You have something for us, I believe?'

'Yes, I've got something for you. But what's all this bloody nonsense about me being arrested?'

'Oh, it's not nonsense, Snow. You haven't been playing the game. You've broken the rules, old chum. I warned you about the consequences of crossing us, didn't I?'

'The bastards,' Snow thought. 'They know about the radio. They've been listening in to me and keeping quiet about it. I'm right in the shit now.'

'We're at war now, Snow. I can arrange for your trial to be carried out in secret. No one will ever know what became of you. You will be executed and your friends across the water will not know. They'll wonder what has become of you, their best agent in Britain.'

'You've got it all wrong. I haven't crossed you. Look here, I said I had something for you and I've brought it,' he stammered, lifting the suitcase on to the colonel's desk.

'Ah, yes,' the colonel said, 'the present.' The SIS man had already made up his mind that no matter what the contents of the case, Snow was doomed. But he had not quite bargained for the sight that met his eyes as Snow unlocked it and opened the lid. There inside was a sample of the latest model of German transmitting/receiving sets. The colonel's eyes lit at the sight of it.

Snow saw the truth in an instant. That gleam in the colonel's eyes betrayed to Snow that the SIS had had no idea he possessed a radio.

'You haven't been monitoring my bloody transmissions,' Snow thought secretly. 'You'd no idea I had a radio. Your detection people didn't pick me up after all. You've showed your hand . . . and I still have the ace.'

The colonel leant back in his chair, his eyes never leaving the radio. 'Hmmm,' he sighed thoughtfully. 'You certainly have come up with the goods, haven't you, Snow? Brand-new, eh? I must say I hadn't expected anything quite like this. A bit early for Christmas,' he said whimsically, 'but a nicer gift I couldn't have had.'

Snow knew then that he had him.

The colonel lifted his eyes from the set and studied Snow for a moment. 'And you've been sending them juicy little bits of info with this box of tricks, eh?'

'Yes, well, nothing very important,' Snow admitted. 'I had to establish contact with them, otherwise they'd have got suspicious. I've tried it out a few times just to see if it works all right.'

'And it does?' the colonel asked.

'Yes, it does. It works very well indeed.'

'Splendid,' the colonel said and rose from his chair. He strode towards a door and opened it. 'Wait in here for a moment, will you, Snow. Just a few things I want to discuss with my chaps then we'll see what's to happen to you, eh?'

Snow went into the room and the door was securely closed behind him. He had seen certain doom and a ray of hope in just a few short minutes and now his mind was in a turmoil of confused thought. The group in the other room talked in muted tones and he could hear nothing of what was said. What they were deciding in there would mean the difference between the noose and freedom. He fumbled for a cigarette, found one, put it in his mouth and lit it, burning a finger as he did so.

At last the door was pushed open and the colonel invited him back into the room.

'Now then, Snow, there is one question I've to ask you. Clearly you had a transmission planned for the near future. They'll be expecting you to keep the appointment.'

'Yes, I was supposed to transmit tonight, or rather tomorrow morning at about four a.m., but I suppose I won't be making that transmission now. They'll know that something's up when they don't hear from me. That will start them thinking.'

'It has also started *us* thinking, Snow,' the colonel intimated. 'You know how we don't like to let people down. It wouldn't do for us to disappoint your friends in the Abwehr now, would it?'

'I don't know what you mean,' Snow said innocently.

'Oh, it's simple. You will make the transmission tonight as planned. I take it you have no objections to that, have you?'

'No of course not but I still don't understand what you're up to.'

'You'll see,' the colonel told him, a sinister half smile returning to his face. 'In the meantime, I think it best that you stay with us for a while, just so that we can keep an eye on you. We wouldn't want you running off so we'll fix you up with a nice comfortable room for two – you and your radio.'

Snow's 'nice comfortable room' was a cell in prison and when the thick metal door slammed shut he still had not worked out what the colonel's scheme was. Unless . . . Slowly the glimmer of truth percolated through Snow's brain and he began to see the colonel's scheme clearly.

The trick was not a new one. It had been used before and very effectively too. The idea was, upon discovering an enemy agent, to arrest him but instead of putting him to death, which was the usual procedure with spies, 'offer' him the alternative of working for the British. Then continue to send information to the

Germans, some of it real but the bulk of it false and misleading. In that way, the enemy could be made to create the greatest blunders by acting on information fed to them by a 'trusted' spy. They could in fact be manipulated by the SIS.

This was Snow's only chance of cheating the gallows. He would have to be seen to cooperate with the SIS and hold nothing back. Thus when the moment of transmission came, he willingly tapped out the prearranged message to Ritter in Germany, telling him that all was well and that he would be transmitting again in the very near future. With that he signed off. The colonel and the others gathered in the cell were well pleased with his work.

'Excellent,' the colonel said. 'You've done well. You'll be required to make some more transmissions then we will relieve you of that onerous task when we can train someone else up in the technique of using the transmitter.'

In the days and nights that followed, Snow sent further reports to Germany, watched closely by one of the colonel's radio men. Each transmission was carefully scrutinised by the SIS experts before Snow was allowed to send off the message and they were satisfied that he was not attempting to tell the Germans something they should not know or warn them that he was not sending of his own free will.

Ritter suspected nothing and the Germans replied to Snow's transmissions without any hint that anything was amiss. But despite Snow's apparent willingness to hand over the radio set there were still those within the SIS who suspected his loyalty, most notably the colonel. The decision as to whether or not he should trust Snow in the future was a difficult one for the colonel. It was clear that Snow would have to continue his personal contact with the Germans. Despite the fact that Britain and Germany were at war, much of Europe was still neutral and unoccupied and therefore it was possible for Snow and the Germans to meet up. Clearly if such meetings did not take place it might give rise to suspicion. In order that the colonel's scheme of deception should stand up, Snow would have to be seen by the Germans to be as loyal and faithful as ever. If his 'arrangement' with the SIS were leaked the whole scheme would collapse.

Snow was equally uncertain of what the future had in store for him. Would the SIS dispose of him as they had threatened, or had the radio changed everything? The colonel had given no indication of what was to become of his spy – until one evening several days later. The door opened and there framed in it stood the colonel. He was alone, unaccompanied by his Special Branch henchmen. He looked directly at Snow, who sat like a condemned man on the edge of the low bunk in the cell corner.

'Very well, Snow,' he said, 'you're free to go.'

'You mean I can – ' Snow began.

'Yes, you're a free man. We've no need to keep you here any longer. We've got what we want. You will remain in the pay of the SIS and continue to work as one of our operatives. It appears I misjudged you, Snow. We need you and can use you.'

The colonel had lied. He no more trusted Snow than he did the Abwehr. He would use him, keeping him on the payroll to give him the idea that suspicion had been erased and that he was to be trusted. He told Snow that he was free to continue working with the Abwehr and that any information he gathered as a result would have to be passed on.

Snow willingly agreed, pledging his loyalty before gathering together his few belongings and leaving the prison.

Outside the air was fresh and clean. He took a deep breath when he emerged from the great prison doors and walked away, too immersed in his new-found freedom to notice the man who followed him. From then on his every move would be watched; he would be the bait. The colonel estimated that the time would come in the near future when Snow might contact Abwehr agents in Britain and when he did, the SIS would be ready. In the meantime Snow had arranged with the colonel to be at instant readiness should his services be required.

Snow rounded a corner and strode across the road towards a bar. Once inside he ordered a large whisky and drank it down in one gulp then he ordered another and retired to a seat in the corner where he sat sipping his drink, wondering by what magic he had managed to escape the executioner. By now the potent scotch was finding its way into his system and he felt better, more relaxed. He went over the events of the past few days in his mind, oblivious of the man who sat at the table beside him with a half pint of beer reading an evening newspaper. Despite his apparently innocent pursuit, his attention was concentrated upon Snow. He watched him order another whisky, drink it, then leave. Outside, another detective took over the tail and followed Snow as he walked through the night towards the railway station where he boarded a train for Richmond. Once home, he was greeted by his mistress who, unaware of where he had been, thought he had deserted her. But there was to be no love-making that night. Snow's appetite for sex was temporarily dulled by the events of the past few days; he was more concerned for his future. The colonel had him dangling on a string like some subservient puppet. He had lost the initiative. Even if he were to make separate contact with Ritter, he knew he dared not reveal that the radio set was now in the hands of the SIS. Friendly as Ritter was towards him, the Welshman knew that if the truth were to become known, certain death would follow. That night, even his favourite scotch failed to subdue his worries and it was a bleary-eyed spy who awoke the following morning to the telephone ringing. He answered it. It was the colonel.

'Snow, I want you up to headquarters immediately. We've got a job for you.'

'Already?' Snow blurted in hangover amazement.

'Yes, get your skates on and get here as quickly as you can. It's urgent.'

Outside Snow's house, sitting in a car about fifty yards from his front door was an equally tired detective. He had been there all night and had been warned that Snow would emerge from the house very shortly. He started the car motor and waited. Twenty minutes later, Snow emerged and began walking along the street towards the nearest tube station. The detective cruised slowly up the road until he came abreast of the pedestrian then wound down the window.

'Get in!' he commanded. For a moment Snow didn't know whether to obey the order or run for his life. In the spy game, one could not take any chances. In spite of the driver's clear English accent, Snow could not be sure whether he was one of the colonel's men or a German agent, sent to whisk him off and dispose of him. Perhaps the Germans had tumbled to the ruse. These thoughts swept through his mind and he was on the point of making a run for it when the voice from the car said, 'Special Branch. Come to pick you up.'

Snow got in and the car shot down the street, bound for central London.

'You were quick,' Snow commented.

'Oh, we're never far off,' the detective replied, revealing to

Snow that he had been under close watch.

'So that's their game,' he thought. 'I'll have to watch it.'

The car negotiated the rush hour traffic of early morning London and found its way to the headquarters of the Secret Intelligence Service where the colonel was waiting.

The interview was short and to the point.

'We've been getting quite a stream of stuff from your friends in the Abwehr. Of course we've kept up our end of things and fed them with some tit-bits to keep them thinking that you're still doing your job. Point is, Snow, that Ritter wants to meet up with you. We'd been expecting this. I don't think he's tumbled to anything but I suggest you pack your bags and make ready to get over to Rotterdam. I've got all the necessary travel permits arranged for you. You're to meet him at the usual rendezvous in two days time so there's no time to waste. In the meantime you'll have to get up to date on the gen we've been feeding him so that you don't make any mistakes when you meet him. Okay? Go on, then, get on with it.'

The conversation was completely one-sided. Snow didn't have a chance to say a word but left with his Special Branch escort to be led to another office where transcripts of all the messages that had been sent were given to him.

Snow looked them over. The SIS certainly had passed on some interesting stuff but it was obvious to someone in the know that much of it was quite untrue. The SIS showed themselves to be a great deal more cunning than Snow had given them credit for. He left the offices and returned home to prepare for the journey. While he was busily packing his bags, his mind was working frantically, searching for a way of keeping faith with the Abwehr.

Snow was still packing when there was a knock at the door. He was not expecting anyone and the sudden knock gave him a jolt. He did not like unexpected visitors and his heart thumped as he went to the door. He opened it and there before him was a face he recognised.

'Evans! What the hell are you doing here? I told you never to come to my place. You bloody clown, what's up?'

Emanuel Evans* was one of Snow's personal agents and a diehard Welsh Nationalist who had proved himself to be every bit as fanatical as Snow – but with one major difference. His

* A fictitious name.

motivation towards treachery was purely idealistic. In the past
he had provided Snow with contacts who had proved immensely
useful in gathering information for the Abwehr.

Evans looked worried and he twitched nervously as he stood
in the open doorway.

'Get inside. Quickly!' Snow commanded, grabbing him by the
arm and pulling him in. Once inside, he turned on the quaking
man.

'What the hell are you trying to do; get me hanged; cock up
my whole set-up? Don't you realise that you might have been
followed?'

'I wasn't followed. I promise you. I've been dodging around
this area for hours and there wasn't anyone on my tail,' he
pleaded.

'Okay, okay, so you weren't followed but why did you come
here?'

'I'm in trouble, Johnny. I had to see you,' Evans said in an
anxious voice. 'I need money and I need it fast. I'm skint. I'm
up to my neck in debt and if I don't lay my hands on a thousand
quid fast, I'm for the high jump. You see, somebody at my place
has tumbled to the fact that I've been picking up bits of information. He found me with secret papers I shouldn't have had. He
put two and two together and now he says that if I don't come
up with a thousand quid, he'll shop me. If he does then the
whole show will be blown wide open.'

'The bastard!' Snow spat. 'Jesus Christ, man, couldn't you
have been more careful? This isn't a game we're playing, you
know.'

'Look, Johnny, I'm sorry, but there was nothing else I could
do. Honest.'

'All right, all right. Here, have a drink, you're shaking like a
bloody jelly.'

Evans took the drink and swallowed it all in one go. He
helped himself to another.

'We've got to think this thing out calmly,' Snow said, composing himself. 'I've had more than my fair share of narrow shaves
these past few days and I could do without any more.'

Snow rolled his glass between his palms as he paced the room,
deep in thought. Outside in the darkened street, a Special
Branch detective found a telephone kiosk. He lifted the receiver
and dialled a London number. The ringing tone sounded only

once before the phone was snatched up at the other end.

'Yes?' a voice said.

In his office at SIS headquarters, the colonel replaced his receiver.

'Splendid,' he thought. 'So far so good.'

The detective left the kiosk and melted into the shadow of a building directly opposite Snow's house to resume his vigil. While the clipped conversation between the detective and the colonel had been going on, Snow's mercurial brain had seen a ray of light that might save the situation and prove beneficial to himself. He could outwit the colonel even now: 'I think I've got it, Evans. I think I've got the answer to our problems. Listen,' he said with growing excitement, 'you travel about a bit in the course of your business. I mean over to Europe to sell your stuff.'

'Yes, but what's that got to do with . . . ?'

'Just a minute. Since you regularly travel abroad there's no reason why you shouldn't make another trip, say to Holland, is there? Holland's still neutral and we're still carrying on trade with her even if she does border on to Germany.'

'Yes, that's true. But what are you getting at?'

'It's like this. I've had a bit of bother with the Secret Service here. I reckon they're on to me so I've got to play it careful for a while until the heat's off. That means that I'm not going to be able to maintain my usual contacts with the Abwehr for a while until the SIS gets off my back. Now this is where you come in.'

Snow went on to explain: 'I want you to take my place for a short while, just so that I can lay low. But it will mean that I'll have to get you over to Holland to meet my contact in the Abwehr. If he agrees to the scheme then you're in business. He'll fix you up with all the money you need to pay off this bloke who's tumbled to your 'other activities'. I can square things with the Abwehr but you'll have to come up with something juicy to get them interested. They've got to see that you can be useful to them. I'll vouch for you but even that won't be enough. D'you think you can do it?'

'Are you kidding?' Evans asked sarcastically. 'My company's got contracts with the RAF. I've got information that'll make the Jerries' hair stand on end.'

'Excellent! Then you're on. I'm going over to Rotterdam in two days. D'you think you can arrange to be there then?'

'No problem,' Evans said confidently. 'Rotterdam it is, in two days' time.'

'Right, then. That's arranged. We'll travel separately. If the SIS have got a tail on me they'd spot you too so we'll leave at different times. I don't reckon the SIS will have anybody shadowing me in Holland so we can meet up there.'

With that Snow thought it time Evans made himself scarce.

'Right, Evans, it's time you weren't here. Ring me tomorrow and confirm that everything's fixed for your trip. You'd better go out the back way. If there is anyone watching the house, they'll not see you leave.'

With that, Evans slipped out the back door of Snow's house and disappeared into the darkness of the blackout. But he had not gone unseen. The curtains of a top floor window in a house which backed on to Snow's were slightly ajar. A pair of eyes peering through the parted curtains creased in a satisfied smile.

The Special Branch was everywhere.

Snow returned to his lounge and poured himself a large scotch. He was well satisfied with the evening's work and he smiled to himself as he sipped his drink, thinking of the day when the Germans would overrun Britain. Then he would have great pleasure in pointing the finger at the colonel and seeing him fry in hell.

While Snow glorified in his masterful ploy to outwit the SIS, Emanuel Evans made for Richmond station where he boarded a train to London. He seemed to be taking a somewhat round-about route to his home but he had a call to make before retiring to bed for the night. There were things to be arranged before he could make the trip to Rotterdam; people to see.

The colonel sat behind his desk in his office at SIS head-quarters. He was working late that night. Under normal circum-stances he would by that hour have been reclining in a chair enjoying a drink at his London club – but not that night. He had important business to attend to. He had an appointment to keep but his patience was beginning to wear thin as he tapped a pencil on his oak desk. Then there was a rap at the door and he called for the visitor to enter. The panelled door opened; in stepped the man the colonel had been waiting for. He sat down and lit a cigarette, inhaled it deeply, then smiled.

'Well, how did it go?'

'Fell for it like a baby, hook, line and sinker,' the visitor replied with a pronounced Welsh accent.

Emanuel Evans sank back in the deep leather chair, pulled again on his cigarette and commented, 'You know, I almost felt sorry for the little bastard. Snow is the personification of everything I despise and he fills me with disgust, particularly since he's a Welshman like me, but he must be suffering the agonies of the damned. He's a man without a friend. Even that dame he's screwing would sell him down the river. She's only after his money and the poor misguided fool doesn't realise it. He firmly believes that he's got you by the short and curlies. He's taking me over to Rotterdam with him to meet his man from the Abwehr. He's even going to put in a good word for me. Looks like this time next week I'll be a fully-fledged member of the Abwehr. Come to think of it, I ought to make a few bob out of it,' he said laughingly.

'Don't be so sure about that, Evans,' the colonel warned. 'Any loot you get from them is to be handed over to us. However, I might be able to arrange a small percentage for you!'

Emanuel Evans, far from being a traitor like Snow, was one of the British Secret Service's best operatives and had been so for some time. When Snow had diligently gone about the business of recruiting key people in the various industries which supplied the armed forces, he naturally approached men who were hard-line Welsh nationalists. Evans was a believer in a Free Wales with its own assembly, but his passionate belief in that stopped very far short of betraying Britain to the enemy. He believed in a Free Wales brought about by a democratic process and he had no enmity towards the English. After all, the Secret Intelligence Service was a *British* organisation, not one peculiar to England and he had been a member of it long before Snow came on the scene.

Little did Snow realise that by taking Evans to Rotterdam to meet Ritter, he was allowing the SIS to penetrate the Abwehr itself. In addition, he would allow Evans to discover how loyal Snow was to the Germans.

The colonel was delighted with the results of that evening's work and throughout that night he and Evans concocted a list of 'secret' information which Evans would give to Ritter to establish his *bona fides* as a traitor to his country.

Within twenty-four hours, both Snow and Evans, armed with

the 'secret' information, were in Rotterdam. That night, the two men were in Snow's hotel room when Ritter arrived. Introductions were made and Snow and Ritter went into an anteroom to discuss whether or not Evans was a suitable candidate for the ranks of the Abwehr. Snow pleaded his friend's case and did so with such conviction that when they finally returned to the room, it was clear that Snow had won. But the cautious Ritter had his own secretive ways of making sure that Evans was no SIS plant.

Drinks were ordered and the three men got down to business. First, Evans was asked to show what he had got and he produced papers which gave details of secret RAF developments. The SIS had gone to considerable lengths to make his revelations credible by inserting some rich but comparatively harmless prizes in the list of information, things which the Germans could confirm with ease. Ritter seemed satisfied then he turned to Snow and asked him what he had got for him.

When Snow had gone through his report, he added some more by word of mouth, information which the colonel back in London would not have allowed him to impart.

Among the information which both men passed on to Ritter there were morsels which Snow knew to be false and he *advised Ritter to discount them* as unreliable. This confirmed beyond doubt that the Abwehr were his true masters, the ones to whom he pledged absolute loyalty, although not for a moment did he allow the conversation to get around to his transmitter except to say that the transmissions were being received.

In due course, Evans was approved and furnished with a code-name. Money was no problem and both men returned to England well endowed with cash. Snow's financial gains were put to his own personal use but the unfortunate Evans had, with some reluctance, to turn his over to the SIS. His report to the colonel included the news that Ritter had given Snow a piece of microfilm which was to be delivered to a German agent who lived in a resort in the south of England. Both Evans and the colonel wondered whether or not Snow would carry out the 'drop' and if so, would he tell the SIS?

An hour or so after Evans had left SIS headquarters, the colonel got a telephone call from Snow. He had something important for him. Snow said he would call within the hour. He did so, bringing the film with him.

Snow handed over the film to an amazed colonel who praised him for his work then quizzed him on what else had happened. Snow related the story of his meeting with Ritter taking great care to omit any reference to Evans and the fact that he had vetted the information that had been supplied for him to pass on to the Germans. Snow left the meeting with the colonel's 'praises' still ringing in his ears.

That microfilm was indeed a worthy prize. It contained the addresses of UK agents of which the SIS had no knowledge and uncovered one of the Germans' mailing points in the shape of a woman living in the south coast town of Bournemouth. She had the task of financing the agents and was subsequently arrested and sent to prison, along with other agents for whom the SIS had no use.

The colonel's suspicions that Snow's loyalty lay firmly with the Germans had now been confirmed and something had to be done about it. By virtue of his business and the contracts he held with the various departments of the armed forces, Snow still had access to top secret information. It was the colonel's intention that that access should be greatly curtailed. He wished to maintain Snow's contact with the Abwehr in order to keep the radio in operation. But above all he had to ensure that any information which Snow might pass on should be of minimum importance.

A few days after their meeting, Snow got a series of shocks which set him thinking – and worrying. The passes which he had been issued for access to RAF stations, military posts and Admiralty establishments were withdrawn 'for security reasons'. If in future he wished to visit any of these secret establishments, he would have to make fresh applications for permission through the usual channels.

Anxious to gather further fodder for his next meeting with Ritter, Snow made the rounds of his contacts in key positions both in industry and in the armed services. Some had gone, while others no longer had access to secret material. One of those he contacted was Evans, who immediately reported Snow's visit to the colonel.

Snow was worried. He had in the past provided the Germans with some truly startling secrets but now it looked as if he would be effectively reduced to a second-rate spy, one who could gather only such information as was visible to the ordinary man in the street.

Snow, to maintain his credibility with the Germans, began a nationwide tour during which he picked up some intelligence about the strength of fighter squadrons at bases throughout the country and pinpointed promising targets for the Luftwaffe. These were useful – very useful – but not the sort of hot tips that the Germans had been used to from their top spy in the UK.

Then Snow pulled off another coup. He made contact with a member of the counter-espionage department, MI5, who was able to furnish him with a detailed list of British agents at work in Europe, notably in France, Belgium and Holland. The exposure of the agents was to be of immense value to the Germans when, a few months later, they were to strike west with all their armed might. Snow passed on this information along with more 'duff gen' supplied to him by the colonel on another visit to the continent.

It was during his meeting with Ritter that he was given a warning. Ritter informed him that this would have to be their last meeting in Europe, and strongly advised Snow not to return because in a very short time Holland, Belgium and France would be transformed into battle grounds. (Ritter made the mistake of confirming this by radio, unwittingly warning the British that Germany was poised to strike west.)

As he returned to England the news of the impending attack on the countries in the West left Snow decidedly glum. It meant in effect that he would have to rely in the future upon radio transmissions and his radio was in the hands of the SIS. It seemed as if this was the end of his career as a spy.

Snow duly made his report to SIS headquarters upon his return to England only to discover that another message had arrived for him, only minutes after his arrival at the SIS headquarters. Ritter wanted to arrange another meeting but this one was to have a novel twist to it. He wanted Snow to find a boat and make his way out into the North Sea where they would rendezvous at a certain point one night in April 1940. For his part, Ritter would arrive at the rendezvous by seaplane. The meeting was absolutely crucial to their operation since Ritter had a job for Snow which was too vital to broadcast. Evans was to accompany him as he too would be involved in the plan.

The colonel realised that whatever it was that Ritter had for Snow and Evans (in the message referred to by a code-name) it must be of great importance and the opportunity of getting it must not be missed.

'You'll go, of course. I'll fix you up with a trawler which will take you to the rendezvous point along with this other agent of yours. By the way, Snow, who is he? It seems that you've been keeping something from us. I want the truth, Snow, otherwise you know the consequences, don't you?'

Snow was cornered.

He was forced to reveal the identity of Evans and he did so.

'I was going to tell you of course,' he told the colonel, 'but there was no point in letting you know before he was firmly established with the Abwehr, was there?'

'Perhaps you're right, Snow. In any event, we'll keep an eye on your Mr Evans. Perhaps the Jerries will give him a present of a radio, hmm?'

'Yes,' Snow said demurely, 'perhaps they will.'

Snow's first priority was to warn Evans that the SIS were on to him and it was now he who dashed to the other's home in a frenzy. Evans opened the door to him.

'Don't say it,' Evans began, anticipating Snow's news. 'You're too late. They've already been. The Special Branch people paid me a visit. Looks like the whole business has been botched.'

'Funny thing, though,' he said with a puzzled look on his face. 'They didn't arrest me. When they came to the door and *told me* what I'd been up to, they just said they would see me again. I don't get it.'

'I do,' Snow said knowingly. 'They're setting you up, mate. They'll use you. You take my word for it. The next thing you know, they'll be putting the squeeze on you to work for them. I know their tactics. They're right bastards. You remember I said they were on to me too.'

'Yes, what about it?'

'Well, I got a visit from them too. That's why I came round here to warn you,' Snow lied. 'They tried to get me to toe the line with them. Seems like they've been tapping my radio link with Ritter and they found out that we've got to meet him, somewhere out in the North Sea. I've got to go through with it but what they don't realise is that I won't be coming back. Things are getting too hot for me here. I'll tell Ritter that I've got to go to Germany with him. And I reckon you should do the same thing. We'll both "blow" and live it up in the Reich. What d'you say, eh?'

'Ritter isn't going to be too pleased about that, is he?' Evans conjectured. 'I mean losing two spies in one go. You know the Jerries. They don't like being let down now, do they? We might meet him at sea and end up in the drink with weights tied around our feet.'

'Don't be crazy,' Snow snorted angrily. 'I reckon we're still worth something to him. Anyway, anything's better than risking our necks here. I'm going on with Ritter and you're coming with me whether you like it or not. Come on, get your gear together. You can stay at my place until it's time to leave tomorrow night.'

Snow's decision to flee the country left Evans in a difficult position. Somehow he had to warn the colonel of the Welshman's intention but throughout the next twenty-four hours, Snow never left Evans's side. He would not allow him even to make a phone call, warning him that 'he wasn't going to make another mistake'.

The next day, Snow got a call from the colonel instructing him to make for Harwich where he would find a trawler waiting for him.

That evening the trawler cast off and put out to sea. Snow had looked decidedly green even before the trawler left port but now he looked positively deathly as the boat was caught in the grip of the sea. Snow had brought along with him a caseful of his finest whisky, obtained on the black market, and he broke into it. Within half an hour the best part of a bottle was gone and Snow reeled more from the effects of the liquor than from the rolling of the trawler.

Snow got progressively more drunk as the voyage continued until he reached a state of utter insensibility. Evans himself felt none too healthy. Like Snow he was no sailor but he had to keep a clear head, knowing full well that a wrong move might ruin everything.

Snow was still unconscious when the boat reached the position at which Ritter was to meet them. The trawler had arrived early and lay at anchor waiting for the sound of the aircraft's engines.

Twenty minutes before the appointed meeting time the evening sky quickly darkened, not with night, but with ominous black clouds. A storm was brewing and in a miraculously short time torrential rain lashed down upon the trawler and mountainous waves dominated it with their towering peaks, throwing it about upon a watery switchback.

Several thousand feet above the North Sea a Dornier float-plane approached the position of the trawler but Ritter finally abandoned all hope of landing, and the pilot headed back to Germany.

Far below, in the teeth of the storm, the time of the rendez-vous came and went. Then the trawler skipper declared that it was pointless waiting any longer and the boat turned back. Throughout all this Snow had felt nothing. He remained deep in the oblivion of drunkenness.

When Snow finally woke, his mind slowly penetrated the agonising mist of a blinding headache and the nausea of a hang-over until he remembered the mission he was on. The boat hardly seemed to be moving. It was rocking gently. He rose from the bench below decks and his head almost exploded with pain. Then he staggered towards the flight of steps and stumbled on to the deck. He could hardly believe his eyes. The trawler was in dock, secured by the quayside. He gripped the railing that skirted the boat and tried to make sense of the situation. In the wheelhouse he spotted the skipper, talking to someone whom he took to be Evans. Walking with great difficulty he made for the wheelhouse and opened the door. Before him stood the colonel.

'Feeling better now, Snow?' he asked with mock concern.

Snow ignored the question. 'Where's . . . ?' he began.

'Evans?' the colonel asked, anticipating him.

'Yes, Evans. Where is he?'

'I shouldn't worry yourself about him if I were you,' the colonel said in a falsely reassuring tone. 'Evans is . . . well, let's say, enjoying the hospitality of the government.'

The colonel's cryptic answer told Snow that his compatriot was under arrest and doubtless in solitary confinement in one of His Majesty's prisons, probably destined to rot there until he met his fate at the rope's end. In truth, however, Evans was fast asleep, enjoying the luxury of a comfortable bed at an address somewhere in London. The colonel had decided to keep Evans 'on ice' for the time being to be re-activated in the future. Snow and Evans would never meet again.

'You don't look quite yourself this morning,' the colonel com-mented with joyful sarcasm.

'It's the sea, colonel,' Snow said. 'I never was very much of a sailor and it blew a frantic gale last night.'

'Yes, so I believe. Pity, that, not meeting up with the Abwehr,

I mean. Great pity. Still, I dare say your friend Ritter will devise some other more successful scheme. We'll send out a message to him tonight telling him that you couldn't make the rendezvous because of the weather, eh? That'll keep him quiet and get him thinking. In the meantime, I suggest you do something about that hangover of yours. Nasty things hangovers,' he concluded with obvious malice.

When Snow arrived back in his Richmond home the house was empty and looked as if it had been ravaged by a maniac. His first thought was that 'it had been 'done over' by the Special Branch, but a closer inspection showed that only two things were missing – his mistress and her clothes. Snow was alone again, friendless, and a world apart from the only people who were sympathetic to him, the Germans.

Johnny Snow, the ebullient optimist, was desolate amid the ruins of a devious life. His misadventures had caught up with him and his booze-befuddled mind could think only of a grim future. Such it seemed was the penalty of double-dealing and treachery. No longer was his life his own. The colonel pulled the strings and Snow had no alternative but to obey. The vital spark that had goaded him on in his unsavoury past was gone. There was no one to turn to – no hiding-place for the failed spy, only the inexorable certainty of an empty future.

In the weeks and months that followed Snow found solace in an increasing daily dosage of alcohol. He was fast becoming a total wreck, careless of caution and still oblivious to the close watch that the Special Branch was keeping on him. Escape to Germany was now hopeless but it seemed that the SIS had lost interest in him. He had heard nothing from the colonel for some time. Then it happened; an urgent summons to the headquarters. Snow rushed to London.

Two nights previously, under cover of darkness, two German agents had been parachuted into England, landing near Salisbury, the picturesque Wiltshire cathedral city. Upon landing, one of the spies had sustained a broken ankle and could not walk. His companion dragged him from their landing-place to a nearby copse where he hid him and tended as best he could to his friend's injury. A crippled spy was a liability his fit companion could not hope to carry. He dared not take him to a doctor for proper treatment. There was only one alternative: radio Germany and ask for help.

In Hamburg, Ritter received the plea for assistance and was quick to act. He radioed Snow, instructing him to meet the fit agent at Salisbury railway station and render all the help necessary to treat the injured spy. Of course the signal did not reach Snow but instead arrived at SIS headquarters. Ritter had quite unwittingly informed the British Secret Service that two more spies had landed in Britain. Not only that, he had also given them their exact location!

Snow arrived at the colonel's office. He had been transformed from an alert little dynamo to a pale-faced, trembling ghost of his former self. He had lost a great deal of weight and his clothes hung on him like cast-offs. He had been a dapper dresser, clean-shaven and with hair glistening with cream. Now he resembled a tramp, gaunt and with large, glazed eyes. He had made a poor effort at shaving and dark stubble showed where he had missed a patch in his haste to report to the colonel. Above his chin were spots of dried blood when he had nicked himself shaving with a trembling hand. The colonel could hardly hide his shock.

For a moment at least the colonel's distaste for Snow mellowed in sympathy but it was fleeting compassion and they got down to business. The colonel briefed Snow on what had happened and told him that he would have to meet the spy as arranged at the station in Salisbury the following day. Then, with the arrangements made, Snow got up to leave. But there was a parting warning for him.

'Botch this one, Snow, and you'll be smoking your last cigarette before a firing squad. You get my meaning I hope.'

Snow understood only too well. He dare not put a foot wrong, for the colonel had warned him that Salisbury station would be saturated with Secret Service men who would make the London rush hour seem like a quiet day at a branch line station. That night and the following morning no drink passed his lips. Snow set off for Salisbury early in the morning and arrived there with time to spare. While he waited outside the railway station, he scanned the faces of the men who went in and out, searching for one that might betray himself as an SIS man. He could detect none of them, but they were there in strength, in the guise of station porters, workmen, postmen collecting mail, seemingly innocent passers-by as well as passengers apparently waiting for a train. The station fairly teemed with them.

Snow already had a brief description of his man; a little under six feet tall, slim, blond and wearing a fawn mackintosh. He was to approach him, ask him for a light to which the German would reply with a prearranged answer.

The minutes ticked by. Snow glanced anxiously at the station clock, then confirmed the time on his own watch. His man was late by a few minutes. Maybe, he thought, something had happened. Maybe the German had already been picked up by a keen-eyed policeman and was already behind bars. Such an eventuality would not please the colonel.

Snow was beginning to despair when a young man, clad in a long raincoat and with blond, almost white hair, walked casually up towards the station entrance and stopped. He looked about himself, as if expecting to meet someone then walked idly up to a time-table and began studying it.

Was this Snow's man? Snow watched for a minute or so. The newcomer turned from the time-table and looked around. Snow could see that there was a look of furtive anxiety about the man. Now he would chance it. He walked towards him.

'Eh, pardon me, but have you got a light?' Snow asked putting a cigarette to his mouth.

'No,' he replied abruptly, 'smoking is bad for my health.'

That was it. Snow had found his man.

A dozen or more pairs of eyes watched the encounter and the departure of the two men as they got into Snow's car – supplied by courtesy of the SIS. With that the mail man clambered into his van; a 'passenger' picked up the phone in a telephone kiosk and made a call to London; a baker's van slipped in behind Snow's car with a veritable convoy of vehicles following after it.

Snow would have given an arm for a drink. His nerves were shattered and it showed. His facial muscles twitched nervously as he drove through the streets of Salisbury.

'Where is he?' Snow asked his passenger, his voice a stammer.

'About six kilometres outside the town. I shall show you the way.'

The German directed Snow out of town and into the country until they took a secondary road which led through the rolling fields of Salisbury Plain. By then, only the mail van was on their tail, the others having broken off their pursuit so as not to arouse too much suspicion. Then the mail van stopped at a lonely farm cottage and Snow's car carried on up a winding track then halted upon the instructions of the German. He pointed to a cluster of trees about a quarter of a mile away.

'I left him there, in among the trees.'

'Right, let's get him.'

The two men made their way over to the trees where they soon found the other spy who by then had given them up for lost. The injured spy writhed in agony on the ground, pleading with his companion to do something to relieve the pain.

'I know a doctor who lives in a village not far from here. He's "safe" and will help us. He doesn't practise anymore. Struck off the register a few years back for unethical conduct but we can trust him. He needs the money. But it would be better if we wait until it's dark before we make a move. Should be dark in another hour or so.'

They waited, the injured man moaning constantly, the other sitting quietly for most of the time while Snow paced nervously between the trees until finally the mantle of darkness shrouded the countryside and Snow declared it was safe to move.

Between them, they managed to get the injured spy to the car and Snow drove off through the night until he reached a small village. No signpost declared its name. These had been removed to fox the Nazis if an invasion ever came. At last, Snow pulled up before a cottage set back off the road.

'This is it. He'll fix you up in no time.'

Snow and the blond spy got out of the car and helped the injured man out of the rear seat and up the pathway to the door. Snow knocked and waited. Moments later they could hear footsteps on the stone floor inside. The door creaked open revealing a grey-haired man with a deeply lined face, hardly discernible in the dim light.

'You're here, then,' he said. 'Come inside quickly. We don't want anyone to see us do we?'

They entered and the doctor pointed towards a door at the far end of the hallway. Snow opened the door and stopped short. Three men stood inside the room, one of them the colonel.

The blond spy spotted them and the revolvers each of them pointed at the trio. Blondie, realising that he had been led into a trap, turned, dropping his crippled friend and lunged at the front door. He wrenched it open but his escape was barred by a Special Branch detective, a burly giant whose massive frame filled the doorway. The detective's clenched fist sank into the spy's stomach. He doubled up and sank to the ground, gasping for breath and clutching his midriff. With one hand, the detective lifted him from the ground and brought him back into the cottage.

When the blond Nazi had regained his wind, he launched himself into a string of oaths directed at Snow, whom he now realised had betrayed him. Snow was visibly terrified as the spy struggled to lash out at him but fortunately for Snow, the spy was securely restrained by the detective. As for his colleague, the broken ankle prevented him from taking any action.

It was a relieved Snow who watched the two men led off and whisked away into the night. For the first time in his life, Snow felt a sense of disgust, having betrayed the two men. He tried to console himself that he had had no option but it was little consolation. Then a new fear came to him. If it were ever discovered that he had been responsible for their fate, the Germans would be merciless in their revenge. But Snow need not have worried. The two spies had brought with them two radios and it was the colonel's intention to use them just as he had done with Snow's. The injured spy fell into the category of the fanatical Nazi and it was realised by the SIS that they could expect no cooperation from him. Since he had not committed any act of espionage or sabotage, he was incarcerated for the duration. The other spy changed his colours with lightning rapidity when the consequences of non-cooperation were made clear to him. Indeed he became a very valuable addition to the SIS and for the remainder of the war kept up the pretence of working for the Abwehr but was in fact in the pay of the British Secret Service. (Bernard Newman, a leading authority on espionage, claims that this German spy married an Englishwoman during the war, had a family, and set up home in London where he still resides to this day.)

Snow returned to the comfort of the bottle but it was not long before he was called upon to keep another rendezvous, this time in London. Part of the arrangement Ritter had made with Snow was that he would receive quite large sums of money with which to finance his own espionage activities and also act as a bank from which other agents could collect money when they required it.

A delivery of funds was due to arrive in London and Ritter contacted Snow by radio and arranged the pick-up. It was of course the SIS who received the message and Snow was sent for. The colonel told him that he was to take a certain bus which passed along Oxford Street at a given time. On that bus would be an 'Oriental gentleman', in fact a Japanese, who would be carrying the money in a copy of *The Times* newspaper. He was the contact and would hand over the money after a few words had established their respective identities. Japan was at that time not in the war but working closely with Germany, helping them in their espionage activities.

The following day, Johnny Snow boarded the bus and sure enough there was a Japanese sitting on the upper deck. Snow sat beside him and asked him casually if there was anything interesting in the paper.

The Jap turned and looked at him.

'You may have it, sir,' he said politely. 'I have finished reading it.'

Snow took the paper and left the bus at the next stop. Nearby was a public lavatory. Snow went in and locked himself in one of the toilets. Then he opened the paper. Between the pages were brand new fivers and some notes of higher denominations – a total of £2,000 in all.

Show's eyes widened in disbelief as he counted out the money. An idea flashed through his mind. With this sort of money he could disappear, buy his way out of the mess he was in. Quickly he rewrapped the money in the newspaper and opened the toilet door. A tall man stood at the urinals buttoning his flies. He turned as Snow appeared.

'I'll take that, Snow,' the man said. 'The colonel didn't get his *Times* this morning and he gets very upset if he hasn't got the crossword.'

Snow's heart sank as he handed over the paper with the £2,000 still intact inside. Gone was his chance of a fresh start, an escape from the manacles of the SIS. He felt claustrophobically hemmed in by the Secret Service, unable to move without someone knowing what he was up to. Trapped!

To add to his misery he was almost broke. His electronics business was failing fast. He could not afford the inflated prices demanded by the black market for his drink and, as his finances dwindled, his appeal to the opposite sex declined. His situation was desperate. He knew it – and so did the SIS . . .

Snow was at their mercy. All the fire of passionate Welsh nationalism was gone. Now he would do anything for anyone. In desperation he went to see the colonel and told him of his plight.

The colonel already knew all there was to know but he listened intently to what Snow had to say. Then he thought for a moment.

'Snow, I do believe there is a little service you can do for us. I have a scheme I've been mulling over in my mind for some time and you might be just the man to see it through. Furthermore, it could get you out of your present difficulties. If you pull it off successfully, it could be worth, say, a thousand pounds to you.'

'I'll do it,' Snow said eagerly.

'I thought you might,' the colonel said knowingly. 'But you'd better know what it's all about before you commit yourself.'

'Well then, what is it?'

'You're going on a trip, to Lisbon to be precise, where you'll meet up with Ritter. When you do, you'll tell him that you've found an RAF deserter, an officer from the technical branch who is willing to sell secret technical information and also act as a spy for the Germans here in this country. You'll persuade Ritter that the officer was cashiered from the RAF on suspicion of having communist sympathies. If Ritter takes the bait then you'll take the officer out to Lisbon on another trip. From then on, it's up to the officer. He'll take it from there.'

'And when do I get my money?' Snow asked. 'I'm broke. I'll need some money to prepare for the trip.'

'Very well, Johnny. We're not tight-fisted here,' he said with a sly grin. 'You can have fifty pounds now, and the balance when the officer is safely delivered and you get back here. After all, we do want you to come back again, don't we?'

This was the break Snow had been waiting for. Thoughts of defecting when he reached Portugal were racing through his mind but the colonel was reading them.

'Oh, I ought to point out, Snow, that you'll be signing your death warrant if you try and cross me. You may be tempted to return to Germany with Ritter. Take my advice – don't. That is, if you want to live. You'll be watched in Lisbon and if you disappear, I'll make sure that the Germans get to know that you surrendered your radio to us and that you betrayed two of their own spies. They don't take kindly to traitors and they have some nasty ways of dealing with double-crossers. The Gestapo are specialists in the art of torture and I'm sure they'd have a field-day with a traitor. You understand your position, don't you?'

'I get the picture,' Snow assured him but he still thought that he could concoct a story that would convince Ritter of his loyalty to the Reich, and in that way persuade him to take him to Germany.

The reunion between the old comrades took place late in 1940 when Snow and Ritter met in a Lisbon café, then retired to an hotel. Ritter was shocked when he saw Snow's condition, and he sensed that something was wrong. His intuition, born of years of service in the Abwehr, told him so, and his suspicions were confirmed by Snow's appearance. There were other reasons too why he had reservations about Snow. In the time since they had last met, Ritter had been able to prove that some of the information radioed to him 'by Snow' had been false, and his mind was troubled. Snow's information had contained nothing of the spectacular that it had done in the past and he was tempted to pension off his 'master spy'.

When Snow broached the subject of his going to Germany, Ritter answered with an emphatic 'no'. Snow would be of no possible use to him in Germany and even the trickle of intelligence that Snow did send him was better than none at all. Ritter made clear his disappointment at the quality of the information he had been getting but Snow countered this by saying how difficult things were becoming in Britain where security was tighter than ever. Ritter was not interested in excuses and was impatient to know why he had been enticed across Europe to meet Snow.

When Snow divulged the reason for his visit, Ritter sat bolt upright in his chair.

'I tell you,' Snow continued convincingly, 'this man knows it all. He was in the technical branch of the RAF until they kicked him out. He's had access to all their top secrets and best of all he's still got contacts in the RAF.'

Ritter was stunned by the news but the veteran intelligence man instinctively sought out a flaw. He questioned Snow endlessly on how he had managed to contact the RAF officer and he checked and rechecked his story. But Snow's replies were convincing and he passed the test.

'Right, Johnny, I want him here. We've got to get him into Germany so that our experts can give him the once-over. But how are you going to get him to Lisbon? Surely he's being watched. Even the RAF wouldn't sack a man with such information in his head and let him slip out of the country.'

'Leave that to me. I have friends in the Merchant Marine who are on the Mediterranean run. They'll bring us over. We'll make it all right, providing one of your bloody U-boats doesn't get us on the way.'

'I think I can make sure that won't happen. Just radio me when you're coming and on which ship and she won't be touched.'

Snow paused for a moment, clearly thinking deeply and wondering if, now that he had revealed the importance of the man he would be bringing, his request to be taken to Germany might be taken up.

'One last thing,' he said. 'There is a condition to this transaction. If I bring this RAF chap over and he proves to be what I claim he is, then I want your assurance that you'll take me to Germany and that I can stay there. Things are getting hot for me in Britain and I think it's time I went to ground for a while.'

Ritter did not even pause to answer.

'It's a deal,' he said firmly, shaking Johnny by the hand. 'And now I must report to Berlin. I shall wait to hear from you. And don't make it too long, will you?'

With that, Ritter left and Snow returned to Britain, his first part of the mission successfully completed. He reported back to the colonel and it was then that he was introduced to the 'RAF officer' he was to take to Lisbon. The airman was Squadron Leader Brown, a purely fictitious identity, but there was nothing fictional about Brown's knowledge of aircraft and their intricate workings. In truth, 'Brown' did have a great deal of knowledge that would be of great value to the enemy but the object in sending him to Germany was to discover just how much the Germans knew about the British Air Force, its aircraft and its strength. Brown's penetration of the Abwehr was a tremendous gamble but one the intelligence services thought worth taking.

While the preparations for their departure were under way, Snow's mind was occupied with his plan to escape to Germany. If Ritter remained true to his promise and took him to Berlin, Snow resolved to betray Brown by revealing his true purpose. The Gestapo would do the rest in extracting from him the information they wanted.

It was a buoyant Snow who set off for Lisbon shortly before Christmas, accompanied by Squadron Leader Brown, but the Bay of Biscay was at its fiercest; a violent storm brought on the rigours of sea-sickness and there was no respite from it for Snow. When the ship finally docked at Lisbon he had to be helped off and it was a pathetic creature that met Ritter at a city hotel.

Snow's voice was weak when he introduced Brown to Ritter. He was ill but not too ill to remind Ritter of his bargain.

'Ah, yes,' the German began, '. . . our bargain. If you remember correctly we agreed that you would come to Germany if Squadron Leader Brown here proved to be the man we wanted. I'm sorry Johnny but I shall have to take him to Germany before his worth can be established. All being well, I shall have you brought to the Reich. The Squadron Leader will return to Lisbon and inform you of the arrangements after his stay in Berlin.'

Snow was disappointed but prepared to bide his time. Later that day, Ritter and Brown left, and Snow embarked upon a marathon drinking binge to while away the time until Brown returned.

The days passed into weeks of round-the-clock drinking until Snow could wait no longer. Throwing caution to the wind, he boldly walked into the German embassy and demanded to see the ambassador. He was refused permission. He pleaded with the receptionist and even revealed that he was working for Captain Ritter of the Abwehr. Finally he was seen by a junior official who promised to contact Abwehr headquarters. A few hours later, the official returned to Snow who had been patiently waiting for a reply.

'I have been in touch with the headquarters of the Abwehr. I must tell you that there is no Captain Ritter and they have certainly never heard of you.'

Snow protested – but it was hopeless. He left the embassy and wandered the streets of Lisbon in a daze. Now he knew. Ritter had never had any intention of smuggling him into Germany. Snow found himself the victim of a double-cross. He remembered the halcyon days before the war; the parties in Ritter's home; the nights of revelry in the Reeperbahn; the heyday of his life as a spy. And now? . . . Ruin and desolation.

Still, there was the rest of the money the colonel had promised him. That gave him a short boost until he remembered that it was payable only if the Brown affair was successful and since Brown had not returned, he had to assume that it had failed.

Dismally, he found his way to the British embassy where a

consular official promised to find him a passage to England on the next available ship.

Some days later he stepped off the ship and was met by one of the colonel's minions.

'Welcome home,' he said with a smile. 'The colonel is most anxious to see you.'

Snow merely nodded and entered the waiting car which sped him to London and the headquarters of the SIS. He trod the familiar path through the labyrinth of corridors to the colonel's room and opened the door. The spy master looked up from the papers on his desk as Snow entered.

'Welcome back, Johnny,' he said in mock friendliness.

Snow's face remained a complete, expressionless blank.

'You owe me nine hundred and fifty pounds, colonel,' he reminded him. But the colonel ignored the observation.

'You look ill, Johnny.'

'Never mind my health. What happened to that bastard Brown?' he asked.

'Ah, yes, Squadron Leader Brown. Good man, Brown. One of the best.'

'Yes, but what happened to him?'

'Happened to him? Nothing *happened* to him. He's quite safe. Been back in London for – let me see – about a fortnight now. He got all we wanted. Thanks of course to you, Johnny. And we're very grateful for all you've done.'

'But he was supposed to pick me up in Lisbon! Why didn't he?'

'Hit a spot of bother getting out of Germany and had to give them the slip. But he's all right now. But forget about Brown. It's you I'm concerned about, Johnny. You don't look at all well. I think you need a nice long rest, away from all this intrigue. Look, I've fixed you up with a nice place in the country where you can relax and take it easy for a while.'

'Yes, but what about my nine hundred and fifty quid?' he demanded.

'Well, old chap, country residences don't come cheap these days. Let's call it rental, eh?'

'You bastard!' Snow yelled at him.

'Oh, come now, Johnny,' the colonel said. 'I could have you shot or hanged. After all, you did try to defect, didn't you? Look, I've laid on a car for you. My driver will take you to your new home. Now, off you go – and take it easy, mind!'

Johnny Snow's country retreat was about as remote as one could get, set in the heart of undulating moorland; a well-built, solid construction of some antiquity, which had been the retreat of many a miscreant in the past. It was Dartmoor prison.

Johnny Snow's 'rest' lasted five years – half a decade of wide-awake nightmares. Within the gaunt, grey walls of Dartmoor prison, he lived on his memories: thoughts of the pleasures, perversions and revelries of a past long gone, unaware that his former master, Admiral Canaris, chief of the Abwehr, had himself been branded traitor and executed by his own countrymen.

When the war ended and dubious peace returned to the world, the studded gates of Dartmoor prison opened to Johnny Snow. He walked out a free man into the mist that perpetually shrouded the moor.

But there could be no freedom for him in the country he had betrayed. He took a boat trip across the Celtic Sea where, under an assumed name, Johnny Snow thawed into obscurity to live a life of exile, shunned and ostracised, paying the penalty of a traitor.

4

A Dane
Called Lassen

The Italian ocean-going liner *Duchessa d'Aosta* sat proud and large by the quayside of a neutral West African port one night towards the end of 1941. There was no moon. Only the liner's bulky silhouette against the dim glow of town lights betrayed her presence. The harbour was mute, disturbed only by the gently lapping water, the far-off drunken din from a seafront bar and the occasional clank of some nocturnal port activity. Otherwise the port was asleep, shrouded and cosy under a mantle of darkness. But not everyone slept that night . . .

Rumour had reached the British Intelligence Service that the *Duchessa* was not the innocent merchant ship she appeared to be, but a supply ship for the German U-boats which scoured the Atlantic. If this were true, and investigation suggested that it was, then as a ship of war she was a legitimate target. But there was a problem. The *Duchessa* was berthed in a neutral port and to attack her there would constitute a breach of neutrality. But the British *had* to put the ship out of commission.

The German captain of the liner felt immune to the hazards of war tucked up in the neutral port. He had no reason to suspect that the British would harm him while he was there. Indeed he felt so secure that, on the night in question, he went ashore with some of his officers.

The still, dark waters of the harbour approaches were disturbed by two small craft sailing in line astern into the harbour mouth. They were tugs, dumpy little craft used to nurse great merchantmen into port, but that night their mission was more sinister. Once inside the harbour their engines fell silent and they drifted forward under their own momentum. One nosed towards

the liner while the other slid close to another suspect ship
moored nearby. On board the tug closer to the liner a young
Commando crouched on the deck, poised, ready to scale the iron
wall of the ship's side. Anders Lassen was far from his native
Denmark and the exigence of war found him a member of the
British Commandos. Now he, along with other Commandos
on the tug, was bent upon subtracting the *Duchessa d'Aosta* from
the German merchant fleet. In the other tug, more Commandos
had similar plans for the other enemy ship in the harbour.

Almost silently, Lassen's tug nudged closer to the liner. The
towering wall of steel grew into a precipitous cliff dominating the
tug. Lassen was charged with a critical part of the operation. He
was to board the ship, taking with him a tow-rope for the other
Commandos to climb.

The tug brushed the side of the ship. Lassen leapt off the boat
and, with the agility of a monkey, grabbed a thick wire hawser
draped over the ship's side and scrambled up. At the top, he
crawled on to the ship's deck. He heard a faint murmur of voices
from below decks and caught sight of a figure at the far end of
the ship.

Moments later the deck of the liner was alive with
Commandos moving like spectres to their appointed tasks. One
slid into the engine-room where a group of black stokers were
terrified at the apparition waving a tommy-gun in their faces.
His instructions were clipped and to the point. Instant obedience
was required, otherwise the tommy-gun would be used. In the
Commando's other hand he carried a 'persuader', a particularly
vicious-looking cosh fashioned out of a twelve-inch-long bolt
covered with rubber. The stokers stood open-mouthed, unable to
protest.

In another part of the ship, the Commando leader, 'Gus'
March-Phillipps, and a few of his men captured the remainder
of the crew. One of them had foolishly tried to resist but a
persuader quickly brought him to heel.

Meanwhile, another group of Commandos set explosives on
the anchor chain and the thick wire hawsers which held the ship
to the shore. At a signal from March-Phillipps, four loud explosions shook the ship and echoed over the harbour and town.
In the engine-room, the coloured stokers leapt with fright, despite the Commando's assurance that all was well. Above them
the hawsers parted but the anchor chain, made of stouter stuff,

resolutely held fast. Lieutenant Geoffrey Appleyard set another charge on the chain and a few moments later, it tore the links in two.

The tug pulled hard on the thick rope which Lassen had secured to the ship and the liner slowly floated away from its berth.

Lassen and the other Commandos on board whooped for joy as the ship slid away from the quay while in the engine-room March-Phillipps 'coaxed' the stokers into getting up steam.

The explosions had been heard throughout the town. Fearing that it was an air-raid, the inhabitants took cover but when no more explosions came they ventured a peep from cover. The sky was dark and there was no hint of the fires and destruction that should have followed a raid. The *Duchessa*'s captain took a drunken, inquisitive look outside. Remembering his responsibility to the ship he made for the docks. But he stopped dead in his tracks when he reached her berth. Perhaps it was the drink, he thought, but he could have sworn that he was in the right place – and there was no ship to be seen. It took a little while for the truth to dawn but when it did, the captain flew into a rage and sped towards the British consulate. There he set about the Consul, pummelled him with his fists and had to be forcibly restrained. He was arrested and imprisoned for three weeks.

In the meantime the *Duchessa d'Aosta* was on the high seas, en route for England. Lassen and his band of pirates, along with an unwilling crew, manned her until she reached Britain. The other group of buccaneers met with the same success and both vessels eventually reached England and were handed over to a grateful Merchant Marine which was critically short of ships.

Stealing that enemy ship was just one of the spectacular achievements in Lassen's clandestine career of Commando operations. He would, in only a few years, become a legend, high on the German 'wanted' list.

There had been a certain inevitability about Anders Lassen's role in the Second World War. As a boy in Denmark, he had shown all the marks of the adventurer. With his brother Frants, he displayed a brand of boyish devilment that left his parents horror-struck. He developed considerable skill as a hunter in the woods and forests around his home and became an expert in the art of stalking. He was a crack shot with weapons of many kinds, particularly with the bow and arrow. It is said that, in his early teens, he could kill a sparrow on the wing with an arrow, a signal achievement, even for an experienced archer. (Many years later as a Commando he proposed the use of bows and arrows on raids but was turned down because it contravened the rules of war.)

After an undistinguished school career, Lassen joined the Merchant Marine and sailed the oceans of the world. Life as a sailor was rough but he loved it. Then came war and Denmark was invaded and taken by the German Wehrmacht. Almost immediately, orders came from Denmark instructing Lassen's ship to make for a neutral port. But he would have none of it and, along with others in the crew, insisted that the ship make for England. He was determined to fight to rid his country of the Germans and to do so he would join forces with the Allies. His captain was opposed to the idea but force of numbers on the ship persuaded him to change his mind and the ship made for a British port in the Persian Gulf.

Lassen thought of enlisting in the Royal Air Force but to his astonishment he was told that there was no call for foreign pilots at that time. Disappointed but still determined, he was offered the chance of signing on in a British ship. This he did. On the *British Consul* Lassen saw action for the first time and this taste of war heightened his desire to get into the fray in uniform. The opportunity came when the *British Consul* put into a Scottish port. There Lassen met Captain Michael Iversen, a Danish army officer who was scouting for young, exiled Danes willing to fight.

Lassen and a band of raw Danish recruits were spirited away to the wastes of Scotland where, in circumstances of the greatest secrecy, their training began. The training was not only tough, it was positively cruel. They were driven to the very limits of their physical and mental endurance. They were fed a diet of gruelling route marches. Mastery in the use of every conceivable kind of personal weapon from the knife to the tommy-gun had to be achieved. Canoeing, rowing and unarmed combat punctuated every day and night. They set about perfecting the technique of the clandestine raid under the ruthless eyes of their instructors. The instructors aimed for reality and to get this used live ammunition. There was no room for mistakes.

At that time two young Commando officers were planning a

brand new unit. They were Captain Gustavus 'Gus' March-Phillipps and his second in command, Lieutenant Geoffrey Appleyard. Both were trained Commandos but saw the great potential in a compact unit carrying out small-scale raids to worry the enemy. They recruited a handful of men and set about training them both on land and at sea. The problem of transportation to the target was overcome when they persuaded the Admiralty to part with a Brixham trawler, the *Maid Honor*. She was a stout little vessel with twin masts and russet sails. She had accommodation for five to eight men, ideal for the size of raiding party March-Phillipps had in mind. As a fishing-boat she was not likely to attract the attention of the enemy. But there was one problem to be overcome. The men March-Phillipps had picked were first-class Commandos but they had little or no experience of handling a boat at sea. He put out feelers to find a Commando with sea training. He found Anders Lassen.

Maid Honor sailed out to West Africa where she was used in searching the coastline for U-boat bases and when the trawler returned to England in 1942 Lassen remained behind, temporarily loaned to another section of the army where he taught Africans the art of commando attack. In England, March-Phillipps looked around for tempting targets. There was no shortage of them and he focused on the Channel Islands, the only part of Britain occupied by the enemy. As soon as the Channel Island raids were given the green light March-Phillipps recalled Lassen. His arrival back in England brought two surprises; he was promoted to the rank of lieutenant and awarded the Military Cross for his courage during operations in West Africa.

More training followed, this time in the rugged countryside of Cumberland before the Small Scale Raiding Force embarked upon its first raids on the Channel Islands and points on the French coast. Among the first was an attack on the lighthouse situated on the rock known as Les Casquets. Intelligence reports indicated that this lighthouse, manned by a dozen men, was being used by the Germans as a naval signal station. It was set on a rock which was perilously difficult to approach, especially at night. Several attempts were made using two naval motor launches but each was thwarted by the swirling sea, high winds and dense fog. Then, a little before midnight on 2 September 1942, the raiders got close enough to launch a small boat.

The tiny boat was tossed high and low until finally by

herculean effort it was brought alongside the towering black rock. With line in hand to secure the boat, Appleyard leapt on to the rock and got a hold. Then the others, including Lassen, jumped ashore. Two men remained in the boat to hold her inshore until the attackers returned.

On the rock, the ten Commandos darted between the shadows heading for their objectives. The door to the eighty-foot light-house was open. The Germans were clearly not expecting visitors. The Commandos swept up the stairs, checking each room as they went. The lower rooms were empty. They climbed higher, moving like phantoms up the darkened spiral stairway until finally they came to a room with a light on. A man sat huddled over a table, engrossed in papers. He had not heard the Commandos approaching until the hammer of a Colt revolver clicked. The sailor turned, alarmed. He saw two men dressed in foreign attire standing almost casually in the doorway of the room, both sporting revolvers. Neither spoke. They did not have to – their errand and intention was obvious. *Ober Maat* Munte's head began to swim. The room spun and he crumpled to the floor. The two Commandos left him there for a moment and searched the room. They found what they had been looking for – code-books and other secret documents. Meanwhile Lassen and the others were rounding up the other Germans, shaking them out of their sleep and bundling them out of bed. Too stunned to resist they came quietly as if experiencing some awful nightmare. Soon they were in the bobbing boat. Appleyard was the last man to jump but as he did so the boat lurched and he missed his footing. The result was a broken ankle, the only injury of the whole mission. The Commandos headed for their waiting launches and were soon on their way back to England.

The raids were kept up and were hurting the enemy, forcing them to move troops from vital areas to guard points the Commandos had attacked or were thought likely to attack. In doing so they weakened their forces in areas of strategic import-ance – precisely the result the Commandos were aiming for. But success was not achieved without a price.

On the night of 12/13 September 1942 Appleyard and March-Phillipps set off with eleven men to raid a point on the French coast. Lassen, who had been on a similar expedition the night before, was left behind, although he tried in vain to persuade March-Phillipps to take him along. To while away the time before they returned he made for the south coast town of Bournemouth to spend the night with some friends. He was in a pensive mood that night unable to relax and enjoy himself. Later he settled down to an uneasy sleep on a couch in the lounge. Then, in the middle of the night, he awoke with a start, yelling at the top of his voice. His worried hosts, wakened by the noise, rushed into the lounge. They found him sitting bolt upright and bathed in sweat. In a nightmare vision he had seen March-Phillipps killed. He got back to headquarters as quickly as he could next morning. His premonition was true. At precisely the same time he had yelled out in the night, March-Phillipps had been killed. The raid had failed and cost the lives of many of the men but Appleyard had survived.

Another raid was planned for the Channel Islands, this time against the small island of Sark. It was to take place one night at the beginning of October 1942. On the eve of the raid, Lassen and the party of Commandos under Appleyard's command set off in a motor gun-boat for their objective. As the boat swept across the sea the weather closed in and she was buffeted throughout the two-hour voyage. The landing area posed a problem. Appleyard had chosen a spot at the base of steep cliffs where there was less likelihood of the beach being mined but his choice heightened the chance of the boat being dashed to pieces on the treacherous rocks.

The Naval navigator did an excellent job in bringing the motor gun-boat as close as he dared before the raiding party launched their small boat and struck inshore. It was a rough ride in to the cliff base but they made it. One man was left in the boat with strict orders to remain where he was until the appointed time of departure. Then he was to leave, even if the party had not returned.

The Commandos were almost a mile from where they suspected the German garrison was billeted and they headed off in that direction. As they progressed, the sounds of the night took on an eery twist. Appleyard and Lassen, veterans of the clandestine raid, knew instinctively which to discount and which to be wary of. They had gone only a few hundred yards towards the barracks when the unmistakable crunch of boots on the roadway reached their ears. Appleyard's hand waved a warning signal and the Commandos faded into the shadows of the road's edge. Moments passed and the uniform tramp of marching feet grew

louder until the raiders could see a German patrol coming along
the road. The temptation to open fire was great but a skirmish
now might well ruin the entire operation.

Crouched in the shadows, they held their breath as the
Germans marched past, chattering in guttural tones and unaware that death was a pace or two away. They were gone as
quickly as they had come, their voices and the sound of their
marching feet lost in the whistle of the wind. With the danger
gone, the Commandos resumed their trek to the barracks.

Ahead, against the dark sky they could just see a cluster of
houses which proved to be deserted. They struck on into a val-
ley. At the other side of it stood a large, imposing house. It was
the kind of house the occupying forces might well have commandeered as a headquarters so it had to be approached with
caution.

The patrol split up and crept towards the house to surround
it. All remained quiet and Appleyard determined to break in.
There was a large french window at the front of the house. He
forced it and slid inside. Ahead of him was a flight of stairs and
while the other Commandos searched the ground floor, he
sprinted upstairs to the first floor and entered a room where an
elderly woman was asleep. He shook her gently and she woke
with a start.

'There's no need to worry.' he assured her. 'I am English. You
will come to no harm.'

'English?' she asked in total disbelief. 'But how . . . ?'

As the realisation of what had happened dawned over her, a
smile of delight spread across her face. She too was English and
had lived on the island for most of her life.

While Lassen and the others stood guard outside the house,
Appleyard questioned the old lady about the activities of the
Germans. The barracks were quite close by she told him, and
most of the Germans would be asleep. Security had been tightened since the first Channel Island raids and the Germans were
resorting to ruthless measures against anyone who helped the
raiders. She showed Appleyard copies of the island newspaper
and proclamations threatening the inhabitants with deportation
to German concentration camps. The possibility of such a fate
befalling her did not seem to perturb her in the slightest. She was
on quite friendly terms with the Germans and in the course of
her travels about the island she had taken note of the positions of

guns and other military installations. She pinpointed them for the Commando who thus acquired a vast store of valuable intelligence.

Appleyard, fearing for the safety of the old lady, offered to take her back to England but she was determined to remain where she was, Germans or no Germans.

The German headquarters was an hotel not far from the house. Appleyard's informer had told him that six or so guards occupied the annex behind the hotel. He resolved there and then to have a look at the hotel and take prisoners if the opportunity arose.

On the outskirts of the town, Lassen and Gunner Redborn were ordered to deal with the guards outside the annex. They found only one sentry outside the hotel.

'I'll take care of him,' Lassen whispered. 'You wait here.'

Redborn watched his companion slither forward towards the sentry's position. A few moments later there was a faint grunt as Lassen's knife dug deep into the sentry's body. He slumped dead on the ground. Without as much as a rustle of the grass, Lassen was back again.

'It's done.' he said. 'The coast's clear.'

He went back to tell Appleyard.

'Right, let's go,' the commander ordered.

The wooden annex was about twelve yards behind the hotel and the Commandos darted spirit-like to the door. The first man there kicked it open. They barged in, tommy-guns at the ready. Inside were five sleeping Germans who were hauled still half asleep from their bunks into the corridor, where they jabbered incessantly.

'Shut them up!' Appleyard barked impatiently.

It took a few digs with knuckle-dusters to quieten them. But still some protested at not being allowed to dress. Again the knuckle-dusters were applied and they shut up. Meanwhile, other Commandos searched the rooms for documents which might be useful to Intelligence. Then, the Germans were pushed outside, where the protests immediately began again and there were scuffles. Appleyard instructed his men to tie the prisoners' hands to prevent them from fighting and attempting to escape.

Redborn was having difficulty with his prisoner who had managed to get his hands free and was pummelling the Commando with his fists. Redborn's man lunged away from him and the Commando dashed off in pursuit to fell him with a rugby tackle. A veritable mêlée ensued with the prisoners yelling at the tops of their voices to rouse their men in the hotel.

'If the prisoners don't shut up – shoot them!' Appleyard ordered. Pickney, another of the Commandos, had had about enough of his German who had wrenched himself free and made a bolt for it. He chased him but, seeing that recapture was out of the question, he shot him.

Back with the main body of prisoners, similar incidents were occurring and the fighting grew in intensity. Another shot rang out, followed by yet another. The din woke the Germans in the hotel and the lights blinked on.

Lassen had two prisoners in a vice-like grip and was not prepared to let them go. While battling with his two charges he yelled to Appleyard, asking if he could throw a couple of hand-grenades through the hotel windows to keep the Germans quiet. Appleyard shouted an emphatic 'no'; Lassen was to keep the grenades in case they were needed later.

Speed was of the essence now. Appleyard decided to make a run for the waiting boat as Germans came pouring out of the hotel, bent upon massacring the invaders. One of the two remaining prisoners were lost in the confusion but the other, by now petrified at the sight of what had happened to his compatriots, did exactly as he was told and they charged en masse away from the hotel with the Germans hot on their heels. At last they bundled themselves and the prisoner into the boat and rowed for all they were worth out to the waiting motor gun boat.

It was only when they were safely on board that they realised they had broken international law by tying the hands of their prisoners. This was forbidden and Lassen, realising what would happen when the dead prisoners were found, volunteered to return to the island and cut the bonds off the dead men. But it was too late. They would already have been discovered.

The following day, the German propaganda machine had a field-day reporting how British Commandos had bound German soldiers before shooting them. What they failed to report was that the Commandos' lives had been at stake and that they were justified in tying up their prisoners. But this did not stop the Germans from taking reprisals: for some time afterwards, British prisoners of war were kept in chains and Hitler ordered that any Commandos captured were to be executed.

Anders Lassen had served a tough apprenticeship in the art of clandestine warfare. He had demonstrated outstanding qualities of leadership, cunning, imagination and determination, all vital to the successful execution of these nocturnal attacks. The odds against surviving these dangerous excursions grew greater as the Germans tightened their security. Losses increased as more and more raids were carried out across the Channel until they reached such a peak that, towards the end of 1942, it was decided that the losses no longer justified the reward from these raids and they were temporarily suspended. But this by no means put the Small Scale Raiding Force out of business. The Commandos were used elsewhere.

Lassen chanced to meet Earl Jellicoe, the son of the famous admiral and a Commando who had set up a unit in the Eastern Mediterranean known as the Special Boat Service. Jellicoe invited Lassen to join the SBS and the Dane jumped at the chance. Before the end of the war Lassen, as a member of the SBS, was to kill or capture more Germans in the Eastern Mediterranean than any other single man.

In February 1943, as soon as the necessary medical preliminaries were completed, Lassen boarded an aircraft and flew to Cairo. He was immediately plunged into another rigorous round of training. Jellicoe, a courageous leader, and his second-in-command, Major David Sutherland, were hard taskmasters and drove the new recruit mercilessly in a specially devised training programme. He was subjected to exhausting route-marches across the desert and transported to mountain ranges for climbing and skiing. He moved on to parachute jumping, swimming and navigation, in both boats and canoes which were to be the craft in which the raiders would get to their targets.

The training period was short but intense and Lassen was eager to get out on an operation. Eventually a raid was planned under Sutherland's leadership against selected airfields on the island of Crete. The invasion of Sicily was imminent and the Luftwaffe were virtually supreme in the air. The object of the raid was to destroy as many aircraft on the ground as possible before they could interfere with the invasion.

On the night of 22 June 1943, the raiders landed on the south coast of Crete at a deserted spot known as Cape Kochinoxos. A reception party waited for them. There were already British agents on Crete who risked their lives by helping the resistance fighters in their struggle against the German occupation force. They were to prove invaluable to Lassen and his party in the days that followed.

The target airfields were situated near the Aegean coast on the north of the island and to reach them, Lassen had to cross a rugged mountain range. The islanders, used to this inhospitable terrain, could negotiate these obstacles with goat-like ease but for the Commandos it was quite a different prospect, especially with heavy packs on their backs, but they forged on until finally, in a state of exhaustion, they made camp for the night.

The following morning, Sutherland divided the raiders into two groups, one to be led by himself and the other by Lassen. Sutherland was to attack one airfield while Lassen was detailed to hit the airfield at Kastelli Pediada, a little way south of Heraklion. Lassen took with him Sergeant Nicholson, a towering Scotsman, two corporals, two radio operators and a Greek interpreter.

The mountain range between them and their goal could only be passed on foot and navigation was all but impossible for anyone other than a native. To overcome this, Lassen had with him a Cretan whose boundless humour was to prove an inspiration to all in the trying days ahead.

With Lassen setting an exhausting pace, which astounded even the Cretan, they thrust into the mountain wilderness. For the first time, Lassen got a taste of the remoteness of command. The success of the raid rested squarely upon his shoulders. He shared the trials of his men but maintained a distance which enabled him to act decisively without fear or favour. Their lives were in his hands and he went about his job with deadly seriousness.

The threat of discovery by the Germans was a constant and dangerous reality. But the Commandos were not without friends. They had willing helpers in every village and hamlet they passed through. The Cretans gave them food: loaves of bread, cucumbers, maize and wine, the best fare they could muster. Sustained by this, Lassen and his men drew nearer to their objective. They dared not sleep in the villages because of the German liking for lightning raids so they took their rest in orchards and caves. After days of trekking, they reached a point ten miles from Kastelli Pediada.

There were still some days to go before the attack so Lassen allowed his men time to relax, but he did not rest. He had first to carry out a reconnaissance of the airfield.

Lassen left his men behind and made his way to a village close by the airfield. He stayed there for several days and nights under the protection of loyal Cretans. Throughout that time he watched the airfield. At any one time there were several Stukas, at least five Junkers, a handful of fighters and some reconnaissance aircraft parked near the east end of the field. But there were formidable obstacles to be overcome if the raiders were to get to the aircraft and plant their bombs. The perimeter of the airfield was ringed by dense barbed wire entanglements while the Stuka dive-bombers in particular were each guarded by three men working in shifts from tents pitched nearby. There were guards at regular intervals along the entire length of the landing-strips. Clearly the runways could not be crossed so an alternative plan had to be concocted and this was where Lassen's cunning came into play. Taking into account the positions of petrol dumps, barracks, hangars and the planes themselves, he decided to make a two-pronged attack. When Nicholson and the others joined him near the airfield, he told them of his plan.

They hid in a narrow cave not far from the airfield. It was from here that the attack would begin. The entrance to the cave was only feet away from the main road along which German vehicles and patrols travelled by day and night but was so small that it could not be seen from the road. Inside the dim cave, Lassen outlined his plan of attack. Nicholson would lead the attack on the aircraft at the east end of the airfield while he and Corporal Jones created a diversion at the west end. In the days that remained until the raid, the men went over the details, perfecting their individual parts in the raid.

Meanwhile, Lassen continued his reconnaissance of the field, keeping it up daily just in case there were any developments which might alter the plan of attack. He donned civilian clothes borrowed from the Cretans and with considerable daring walked right up to the wire surrounding the airfield for a close look.

The deadline for the attack was the evening of 4 July. Lassen had agreed with Nicholson that the attack would be made simultaneously at 23.30 hours. A few hours beforehand they made their way to the airfield and lay in wait.

While Nicholson and his men went round the airfield to the east end, Lassen and Jones lay in a vineyard overlooking the field. They could see their objective in the half-light. German and Italian guards walked about the aircraft which sat squat and black at the far end, while beside them were tall hangars with more guards pacing their beats among the buildings. These were to be Lassen's targets.

The seconds ticked by until, a little before 23.30 hours, Lassen and Jones moved out of their cover and down towards the airfield. Lying prone by the wire, Lassen got to work with the cutters while Jones kept watch. The snap of the cutters biting through the wires seemed to echo across the airfield but astonishingly was not heard by the guards nearby. After a few tense minutes, Lassen had made a hole large enough to allow them through and they were soon on the business side of the wire.

An Italian guard emerged from the shadow of a hangar. Lassen leapt at him like a cobra. He cupped his hand over the Italian's mouth and plunged his knife into the man's body. He was dead before he hit the ground. With the guard silenced, Lassen and Jones moved on. There was another sentry not far off but at this stage Lassen did not want to raise the alarm and he resolved to try and bluff his way past him. He and Jones marched purposefully towards the guard who automatically challenged them. Lassen, a fluent German speaker, answered in the guard's native tongue and they were allowed to pass. So far so good. Another sentry stood between them and the hangars which Lassen intended blowing up and again their bluff worked. In the darkness one uniform was much the same as another and Lassen's command of German did the trick. A third sentry was similarly fooled but the fourth was not. He began to raise his rifle but before it got farther than waist-high, Lassen fired from the hip, felling the German with a single shot. The sound alerted the whole airfield. In a moment, guards were charging wildly about, a siren wailed and flares lit up the western end of the airfield.

'That's done it!' Lassen yelled. 'Let's get out of here.' The noise of battle grew into a deafening din as Germans and Italians mistook each other for the enemy and fought a pitched battle. The merest shadow caught the full fury of the fire and, under cover of the chaos, Lassen and Jones found their exit in the wire and slithered through it. Outside they met up with one of their Cretan guides.

From a vantage point on the perimeter, Lassen could see that pandemonium was complete. Throughout all this, Lassen's thoughts were with Nicholson at the other end of the field, hoping that his diversion was working and keeping the guards busy while he planted his bombs.

For almost half an hour Lassen and Jones lay watching the action, then it died down. This is what they had feared. Lassen decided to go back on the airfield again to stir things up and give Nicholson more time to plant the bombs. Once more he and Jones slid through the wire. They scrambled towards a hangar and Lassen was in the very act of darting into it when he was spotted. This time the guard was the first to fire but luckily his aim was off and the bullet whined past Lassen's head. The crack of the shot brought other guards racing to the German's aid. Lassen yelled to Jones to run for it and they sprinted off into the night, losing their pursuers. Fighting for breath, they found themselves in a quiet part of the airfield but, within seconds of getting there, a tracer zipped past the two men. Nowhere was safe. They bolted again for the hole in the fence but this time they could not find it. There was no time to search so they pushed themselves under the barbed wire, ripping their clothing in the process.

Both men fled into the security of the night but they had gone only fifty yards when they charged headlong into a German anti-aircraft battery.

'What's going on?' the German battery commander demanded. Lassen's reaction was swift.

'The British!' he said breathlessly in German. 'The British are attacking the airfield. Fire your gun at the field. Come on – open fire before they take the field!'

The encounter lasted only a few moments and Lassen and Jones were gone but, as they disappeared into the night, Lassen noticed that the gun was being turned on to the field. With their lungs almost bursting from the exertion, they flopped down at a point overlooking the airfield and surveyed their latest handiwork. But Lassen was still not satisfied.

'Come on,' he said. 'We're going back. I know it's chancing our arm but it's got to be done.' Jones merely nodded. He would have followed Lassen anywhere.

Once more they found their way through the wire and made for another hangar close by. By now the defenders were firing at anything that moved and their sights focused on the two intruders. Guns opened up from all directions. A machine-gun sprayed a hail of bullets at them with uncomfortable accuracy. Lassen knew that they would lose a scrap with them and they ran once more with bullets whining about their heads. Luckily neither of them was hit and they fled into the comparative security of a dark patch. But Lassen was not done. He caught sight of a tractor and stopped to plant a bomb on it. This done he ran on again and had taken only a few strides when he realised he was alone. Jones had disappeared. He had clearly not stopped when Lassen broke his flight to plant the bomb. He searched for Jones but could not find him and elected to get out of the airfield in the hope that Jones had done likewise. But when he reached the wire and crawled through there was no sign of the corporal. The awful thought that Jones had been taken prisoner struck Lassen and he determined to return to the field once more and make sure.

Again, Lassen slipped through the wire and crept across the perimeter towards a group of soldiers standing guard. He slipped so close to them that he could hear them speaking quite clearly and surmised from what they were saying that no prisoners had been taken. Jones must have made good his escape so Lassen made his way back to the wire and struck out into the darkness, confident that by now Nicholson and his men must have planted their bombs.

Nicholson's group had its moments of high tension, despite Lassen's valiant and almost suicidal diversion. With the fuses on their time-bombs already running out they had made their way through the wire and begun setting the bombs on the planes. One by one they found their targets and darted around the hangars and parked aircraft depositing their bombs. The intensity of the fire from Lassen's end of the field was such that Nicholson felt sure Lassen and Jones had been killed or captured, and when all the bombs had been planted, he headed into the mountains without waiting to link up with Lassen. They had no sooner crawled through the fence than the whole east end of the airfield erupted in a series of violent explosions. Aircraft disintegrated and hangars were transformed into blazing infernos which illuminated the whole area. They had done their jobs well but now they had to make good their escape and they dashed like hares up the mountainside. The defenders of the air base soon gathered their wits and in minutes searchlights began sweeping the mountainside, catching the escapers in their pencil-thin beams. But Nicholson had the measure of them. Whenever a searchlight caught them they froze to the spot and by doing this remained unseen by the Germans.

Lassen had found no sign of the missing Corporal Jones and when dawn came he knew he would have to hide up for the day to avoid German search-parties. Lassen could find no better cover than a field of cabbages where he lay flat and consumed several fat vegetables. That night he made further headway but he was faced with the same problem the following day. He opted to lie out in another field, this time planted with a crop of onions which he tucked into with distaste. The day wore on and the burning sun beat down on him, scorching his face. Without water or shade he began to suffer the effects of sunstroke. It was then that the noise of footsteps reached him. He raised his aching head and peered in the direction of the sound. A peasant was walking his way. Discovery was inevitable so Lassen took the initiative. The Cretan showed no surprise when the ragged Commando grew from his field. Lassen told him who he was and the old man led him to a village where, to his delight, he found Corporal Jones and the Greek guide.

Lassen was surprisingly fit after his ordeal but his burning thirst could not be satisfied despite the fact that he drank eight or nine bottles of water. Moreover, the onions had upset his digestion and he had an uncomfortable few days while he made his way to the coast led by a band of Cretans which grew in size at every village they passed.

The trek across the mountains passed without event and they reached the coast where they met up with Sutherland and the other patrols which had returned safely having met with some success in their raids. But there was trouble looming. The Germans, realising that they could never hope to find the saboteurs in the mountains, sent their troops to the south coast, knowing that the raiders would in all probability re-embark there on to the ships that had brought them. The boats were not due to pick them up for three days and, when reports arrived that massive German forces were on their way there, Sutherland was worried. The Cretans who had accompanied Lassen were itching for a fight but Sutherland wanted to avoid a clash at all costs. They had achieved their objective and there was no point in risking their necks further at this stage of the game. Sutherland therefore spread his men out over the area so that they would not be caught in a concentration. Soon two Germans were reported in the vicinity and they wandered into Sutherland's area, where both were quickly captured and taken prisoner. Shortly afterwards, two more Germans appeared but they walked straight into the sights of the Cretans who were armed with primitive muskets and weapons of unknown vintage. The excited Cretans opened fire, alerting the other Germans. Sutherland was horrified and instructed Lieutenant Lamonby, a close friend of Lassen, to get to the Cretans and stop them firing. Lamonby managed to put a stop to the firing and then chased after the Germans who had fled the scene. Not long afterwards, the sound of a shot shattered the stillness. The Commandos waited tensely, hoping that Lamonby would return. But, as time passed and there was no sign of him, it seemed clear that he had been killed. But Lassen was determined to find out what had happened to his friend and he set off in search of him, accompanied by a sergeant.

Lassen yelled at the top of his voice in the hope that Lamonby might hear him but no answer came. They searched high and low but still there was no sign of Lamonby. Lassen had to give up. Lamonby was later found dead by a British agent.

At last at about three o'clock in the morning the dull throb of ship's engines reached the Commandos' ears. The Navy had arrived and soon they were all on board, en route for Cairo with the jubilant raiders secure on board. But on Crete the Germans were exacting a toll for the Commandos' success. The General commanding the island took hostages. Fifty-two souls were dragged from their homes and executed. He went on to threaten that if the British agents whom he knew were hiding out in the mountains were not surrendered to him, a further fifty hostages would be shot.

For his part in that raid, Lassen was awarded a second Military Cross. For him, the Crete raid was just the prelude to a saga of adventures in the eastern Mediterranean. Few occupied islands in the Aegean escaped Lassen's attention and his name very quickly became an object of fear for the Germans. A reward of twenty thousand marks was offered for his death or capture. But no one was tempted to betray him.

Lassen was a master of the art of improvisation and, no matter how tight the spot he found himself in, he would find a way out that invariably cost the enemy dearly.

The Italian surrender following the invasion of Sicily and the mainland by no means meant peace in the Aegean. The bulk of the Italian army welcomed the surrender but there were still die-hard Fascists to contend with, particularly in the Dodecanese. The ordinary Italian soldier would fight for the Allies or at least offer no resistance, were it not for the Fascists. The Germans regarded the common Italian soldier with contempt and, where there were islands occupied by both Italians and Germans, the Allies could expect little help from the Italians. But some of the islands were exclusively Italian-held and it was to those that the Special Boat Service was sent to determine whether or not they could count upon the Italians for support.

On the evening of 17 September 1943, two motor gun boats swept towards the small island of Simi which lies not far from Rhodes, the principal Dodecanese island. The island lay dark and still. On board his boat, Lassen peered towards it for signs of life. The island was his objective and it was to be taken and held, with or without the help of the Italians. The assault was under the command of Major Jock Lapraik who had to find out how well defended the island was and whether or not the Italians there were sympathetic towards them. They might, under pressure from the Fascists, make a fight of it. Lassen was the obvious choice to make the necessary reconnaissance expedition and he set off in a canoe with Sergeant Pomford.

As they paddled towards the shore, both men became aware of the sound of bells. They paused for a moment and listened. It occurred to him that the bells might be some sort of warning signal from observation posts on the cliffs. They could have been spotted. The tinkling bells continued and then it dawned on him – they were goat bells. Relieved, they pressed on into a bay in which lay the town of Simi. They pulled in to the shore at the base of the cliffs and hid the boat before setting off.

As they slipped in among the houses they could hear the sound of music. Cautiously they made their way into the main street. It was crowded with people, and the cafés and bars in the town were packed. Lassen and Pomford had taken only a few steps when their uniforms were spotted and recognised as British. It was the signal for great jubilation and in the space of less than a quarter of an hour the entire population of Simi knew that they had arrived. The inhabitants took the Commandos for a liberation force and every church bell on the island was rung.

The din reached the two boats waiting off the bay. Lapraik had no idea what Lassen was up to and could not understand.

There were about one hundred and fifty Italians on the island who heard the pandemonium and came to investigate. Lassen went to work in earnest and told the commander in no uncertain terms that he was to surrender or suffer the consequences. The Italian, imagining that the entire British fleet was standing off-shore waiting to bombard his island, surrendered without protest. Lassen had now to determine the depth of the harbour and asked a group of Greeks if they could help. The Greeks erupted in a confused and incomprehensible babble. Exasperated, Lassen threw himself fully-clothed into the harbour. He disappeared out of sight and a few moments later reappeared and yelled to Pomford to signal the boats and let Lapraik know that the harbour was deep enough.

When the boats arrived, Lassen took some of his men and occupied the best defence point in the bay – a schoolhouse inside a fort overlooking the town. From this vantage-point he could see the entire bay and across the mountain range to the other coast.

Lapraik and Lassen discovered by interrogating the Italians and with the cooperation of the Greeks that there were no Germans on the island but there were German garrisons on near-by islands which meant that there was a distinct possibility that they might try to take Simi. Both men realised that they could not hope to hold the island against a determined German attack and persuaded the Italian commander to put his troops at their disposal. Together they might have a chance.

For almost a month, the SBS, largely under Lassen's command, carried out reconnaissance missions on the islands near to Simi, using caiques to transport them. These excursions were made to determine whether there were any Germans in the vicinity. The missions were particularly daring, for Lassen led them in broad daylight to get the best possible view of the islands. To his relief, he found that most of the islands had been deserted by the enemy. On one island, Calchi, Lassen discovered a twenty-millimetre gun which he promptly purloined for himself. It was not in perfect working order but that was soon rectified by the local blacksmith when he returned to Simi. It became Lassen's pride and joy and he placed it outside his headquarters.

A few days later, Lassen learned that German troops had occupied Calchi. He determined to find out the strength of the new garrison and set off with a group of men. He landed at night on a desolate spot on the coast and led his men towards the town. Some peasants they met told them that the Germans had already gone, depleting their meagre rations in the process. The islanders were starving, for the Germans had taken what little food they had. Lassen also learned that there were Italians on the island who had been brought there by the Germans and he saw an opportunity of increasing his forces. The young Dane's powers of persuasion were immense and the following day he recruited all twelve of the Italians as a defence force against the Germans – a formidable accomplishment considering that the Italians' sole desire was to get out of the war. Reviewing his new troops, Lassen saw at a glance that they were far from fit and put them through a brief but intensive course to bring them up to scratch.

Between these exhausting bouts of training, he had them build stout defences on the island. He equipped the islanders and the Italians with both ammunition and weapons and gave them as much food as he could spare. By then he was far from well. During his stay, he had suffered severe burns on his legs and the medical orderly advised him to leave and return to England for treatment. Lassen would have none of it. Instead, against all advice, he went on another reconnaissance.

Back on Simi, we waited for what seemed the inevitable German attack. The first warning came when the neighbouring island of Kos was raided by the enemy. The long periods of watchfulness were having a detrimental effect upon the health and morale of his men so Lassen ordered them to stand down and the sentry duty was taken over by RAF personnel who had arrived on the island fresh from Cairo. As luck would have it, it was on that very night that the Germans launched their attack.

At dawn on 7 October a boat-load of one hundred and fifty storm troops landed in Pedi Bay. Their arrival went unnoticed by the RAF men and the result might well have been devastating had it not been for Lassen.

The first clashes took place not long after the landing and the island reverberated to the sound of shooting. No alarm had been raised but Lassen quickly gathered together his men and briefed them to search the island and discover the scale of the attack. He could rely upon the islanders to put up a fight but the Italians were an unknown quantity. He had no idea where their loyalties would lie when it came to a fight. But it was the Italians who took the initiative and fired a flare.

Lassen darted through the labyrinth of narrow, cobbled streets in the town, unaware that the Germans had already made some gains by capturing positions in the mountains. Their successful initial thrust instilled confidence in the attackers, but they made a serious tactical error when they sent men into the town of Simi itself.

Lassen had with him Corporal Sean O'Reilly, a towering giant of an Irishman who had appointed himself Lassen's body-guard and followed him everywhere with leech-like attachment. O'Reilly was a scrapper none could beat and a constant source of trouble for Lassen when off duty; but in a fight there was none better to have by his side than the Irishman. They were discussing the situation while creeping along one of the narrow streets when Lassen stopped in his tracks.

'Germans!' he said urgently, holding O'Reilly back. The Irishman could see none but Lassen had some sixth sense that told him they were near. They crept forward to a wall and peered over. Sitting on the other side were two Germans. Lassen did not hesitate but loosed off two rounds over their heads and they surrendered, trembling with fright. Now that Lassen knew they were in the town, he hurled himself through the streets, striking at the Germans with the speed and suddenness of a thunderbolt. He ran headlong into some, firing from the hip and felling them before they knew he was there. Others fell to him after he had stalked them with the cunning of a hunter.

The troops and Greeks were bewildered at Lassen's Will-o'-the-wisp appearances. One moment he was there then he was gone, only to appear again moments later. He was seen all over the town and where he went, Germans died. He accounted for whole patrols penned in by the narrow corridors that were the streets of Simi. He took a fearful toll of the enemy and the ferocity of his attacks stunned them. They fought with determination in a bid to reach the fort on the hill and gain the advantage of height but Lassen and his men barred their way with a withering hail of fire. The enemy was held but Lassen learned that all was not going well in the mountain range behind the town. As he had feared, the Italians detailed to hold the range had succumbed and fled before the Germans. Fascists were tracking down the Italians in a bid to get them to surrender to the Germans. Lassen followed and found them in full retreat. He decided there and then that he could only convince them to stand and fight by example. He began by hunting down and capturing a German sergeant and two privates. O'Reilly was less subtle and cut down three Germans who were chasing the Italians.

The battle raged on through the morning and into the early afternoon with Lassen in the forefront throughout it all. The Germans had taken a terrible beating, despite their superior numbers and they called in the Luftwaffe to help. Three Stuka dive bombers plummeted down on Simi with sirens wailing and bombs thudded into the houses. But still the Commandos and the Greeks fought on with lethal determination. By mid-afternoon, it looked to Lassen as if they had won the day as he observed the fighting from a vantage-point in the fort. But his hopes were dashed when another menace arrived, a boat-load of German reinforcements. From the schoolhouse in the fort Lassen saw the boat approach and he knew immediately what had to be done. The twenty-millimetre gun he had taken from Calchi was several yards away. It stood on the fort wall but between him and the gun there was no cover. Undeterred, he dashed over to it, swung it round, fired towards the boat which was landing the Germans in the bay, and flung himself back into the school-house. After a short pause he was out again and firing at the boat as it bumped against the shore. Again and again he emerged, braving small-arms fire which lashed the open ground between him and the gun, to fire more and more accurately at the German boat, scoring several hits. Finally the Germans could take it no more. Realising that the opposition was too stiff for them they turned tail and fled. The sight of the departing reinforcements made the other Germans realise that the battle was lost and they made for the coast where they were evacuated. The total number of Germans Lassen killed that day is not known, but he found sixteen dead and some thirty wounded, most of them the result of his action. In addition to this there must have been casualties on the boat he had attacked so murderously from the fort. But for Lassen's single-handed action, the island would have been overwhelmed by the invaders. For his part in repelling them he was awarded a third Military Cross.

There followed a fierce and almost continuous aerial assault upon the island by the Luftwaffe and it became clear that it would continue for as long as the British remained there. It was therefore decided that, in order to spare the islanders from further attack, the British forces would withdraw. A week later, however, Lassen was on his way back again. Information had been received from the island that all was not well. It came from the Abbot who lived in the island's monastery. Italian Fascists had been active again so Lassen landed on the island, captured eight of them and wrecked the radio station.

But after Lassen left, he learned that the Italians had murdered the Abbot and the radio operator who had been filtering information through to the Allies from the island. Lassen was furious and demanded that he should be allowed to return to the island. Permission was granted and he exacted revenge by killing an Italian officer and two of his men and by destroying an artillery position.

Lassen, by then a captain, was subsequently promoted to the rank of major and his dynamic raiding continued unabated throughout 1944. He fought in the Aegean again, in Greece, Yugoslavia, in Italy, from a base in Turkey and again in Crete before returning to Italy to help mop up the last of the Germans fighting in the north.

In the north-east of Italy, not far from the city of Ravenna, lies Lake Comacchio, a vast expanse of shallow water separated from the sea by a narrow strip of land comprising mostly sand dunes. The lake itself represented the edge of the right flank of the advancing Allied army but the slender neck of land was heavily defended by the Germans. It was estimated that if the strip of land could be attacked from the lakeside there was a good chance of routing the defenders and throwing the main German line off balance. Field-Marshal Alexander regarded the taking of this land as of the utmost importance and the job was given to a Commando force with the support of the Special Boat Service. Anders Lassen was appointed to lead the support group and at the end of March 1945, he reported to Brigadier Tod, the Commando leader.

Tod, with his Commandos, was to establish a bridgehead on the western shore of the lake and Lassen's job was to cause a diversion by launching an assault upon another area on the same night as Tod's attack. Before this, though, Lassen was to carry out a reconnaissance of the lake to determine where the deep water channels were so that he could lead Tod's forces across the lake. Throughout the following week Lassen spent every night on the lake, venturing dangerously close to the German positions and one night actually risking a walk into the town of Comacchio itself. He scouted around the small, flat islands that dotted the lake and was able to give Tod a complete picture of the obstacles that would lie in his path.

On the night of 30 March thirty canoes slipped into the water of Lake Comacchio. Each carried two men and with Lassen in the lead they struck out into the lake, their objective to capture and occupy the small islands far out in the lake. The going was tough for each canoe contained weapons, food and ammunition and some carried radio sets.

From the shore, Tod's Commandos watched as the canoes slipped away into the darkness. They had six miles to cover before they would reach the islands and they could not be sure of the extent of the enemy opposition there. But Lassen was prepared for a bitter fight. The success of Tod's whole operation hinged upon his taking and holding the islands.

The mass of Lake Comacchio is barely two feet deep and punctuated with mud-flats which proved troublesome obstacles for the canoes as they nosed out into the lake. Hitting one meant getting out of the canoe and shoving it over the bank before clambering back in and rowing it. It was a messy and frustrating experience which shortened tempers at a time when they all had to keep their heads. One of the canoes turned turtle, disgorging the party's rum ration and a radio set.

Finally they reached the island of Casone Agosta, a flat, desolate patch of land with no trees or houses. It was deserted and Lassen decided to camp there for the remainder of the night before launching his attacks the following evening. All the canoes were hauled up on to the island and hidden beneath gathered bracken. With no cover to hide them from the prying eyes of the Germans in daytime, the party was forced to lie flat and motionless throughout the entire day. It was an aching, stiff-limbed bunch of raiders who stretched their legs when darkness took over the island once more.

They left and headed for the largest island, Casone Caldiro. Once ashore they crept towards two houses not far from the shore, which turned out to be empty and the men looked forward to a warm night's sleep – but Lassen had other ideas. He judged that if the Germans had got a hint that they were there, they could easily shell the island from their positions onshore so he took his men to a spot some distance away from the houses and they dug in.

Dawn came and the day passed without the expected bombardment. The Germans had clearly not realised that the islands were systematically being occupied by Lassen's force. So Lassen allowed some of the men back into the houses where they bedded down. But during the night that followed, boat-loads of Germans passed close by. Captain Stellin, occupying a smaller island, ambushed the boats and brought five prisoners to Lassen. It was a fortuitous capture for the Germans had with them a stock of wine, which the Commandos shared with them. The Germans were then locked up in the house but during the night one of them escaped. When dawn came they saw a boat drifting not far from the island. When it was retrieved, they found the German slumped in it. He was dead. What had happened to him was a mystery.

A little later, a boat arrived bringing the party fresh supplies of water and ammunition but this had no sooner been unloaded than the island became the target for a fierce artillery barrage from the German lines. The shelling continued throughout the day and was lifted at six in the evening. Fortunately the casualties were light and that night the wounded were taken off. The following morning, however, the shelling began again, directed not only at Lassen's island but also at smaller ones nearby. It transpired that the Germans had an observation post which had a near perfect view of the islands and whenever one of Lassen's men moved, another salvo of shells was fired.

As the islands were thrashed by fire, Lassen's anger grew. Something would have to be done to alleviate their plight. He signalled to Tod asking him to send over Commandos to occupy the islands while he and his men carried out a raid on the German lines at Comacchio.

The Commandos arrived a little before dawn on the morning of 8 April. The bombardment was resumed and continued unceasingly throughout that day. After nightfall Lassen set off for Comacchio with his canoe-borne raiders. He had divided them into three groups, one which he led himself, the second under the command of Lieutenant Turnbull and the last led by

Stellin. Lassen's and Turnbull's patrols were to land about a mile and a half south-east of Comacchio and make their way up the road towards the town, while Stellin's patrol was to land farther to the north-west.

Lassen did not know the strength of the enemy at his landing-point and was braced for a bitter encounter. The Comacchio road lay by a small dam with water on either side. On the east side the Germans had flooded a wide expanse of land while on the other side there was a canal which ran along the edge of the road and was separated from the lake by a dyke.

Lassen and his men had gone no more than five hundred yards along the road when a challenge echoed from a fox hole ahead. They stopped dead. Fred Green, who was immediately behind Lassen, answered in Italian and told the Germans that they were fishermen returning from their work. The ruse worked and they were allowed to pass, seen by the Germans as only vague shapes in the darkness. Lassen and his section of the patrol were past the fox hole when another shout came, demanding that they come back. The Germans had heard the remainder of the patrol and grown suspicious. Green moved forward to speak once more but immediately a machine-gun in a pill-box behind the fox hole raked the road with fire, hitting some of the men. They dived for the cover of the slopes on either side of the road but it was pitifully inadequate and the German gunners made more hits. Pill-boxes farther up the road joined in the fire. Lassen acted, charging forward alone and slinging grenades through the slits in the first pill-box. A violent explosion wiped out its occupants. Then Lassen led his men in a hand-to-hand attack on the fox hole where they dealt with the men in there.

A little way farther up the road, about six machine-guns in the German pill-boxes fired accurate bursts along the road. Barely an inch of the road escaped and Lassen knew that if he were to extricate his men from this jam he had to do something – quickly. Oblivious to the whining bullets, he leapt out of his cover and ran full-tilt up the road, firing from the hip and tossing grenades through the slits in the first pill-box he came to. In an instant, it erupted, killing the Germans inside. But he had not finished. He sprinted on from there, pulling out two more grenades and, through a wall of fire, reached the next pill box and hurled the grenades inside. A loud boom sounded from within it and belching smoke puffed out of the slits. The Germans were dead.

The confusion caused by Lassen's lone, lightning attack gave him time to dart back to his men, crouching by the roadside. In the pause, he ordered his men to follow him along the road. But they had not gone far before the enemy opened up again from more pill-boxes. The bullets cut into the patrols and Very lights brought daylight to the scene, exposing the raiders. Lassen took no notice and, while the patrols hurled themselves for cover, he remained upright, blazing away at the pill-boxes and continuing to throw hand-grenades at them. Meanwhile, his men were falling wounded behind him. Lassen, out of grenades, dashed back for a fresh supply and ordered his men to take up positions behind a rise at the roadside and aim their fire at a pill-box ahead. He determined that he would wipe it out and with Sergeant Major Stephenson and O'Reilly behind him, he belly-crawled towards it with bullets from friend and enemy whipping over his head.

Reaching a point opposite the pill-box where there was a little cover, Lassen ordered Stephenson to hand over all his grenades. He would launch the bombardment *himself*. He would not have his men subjected to any more fire than was necessary. With an armful of grenades, he stood bolt-upright and began tossing them in the direction of the pill-box. After several had exploded and the dark shape of the pill-box had been completely shrouded in smoke, a yell came from it. It was just one word – 'Kamerad!' Lassen took this to mean that they were surrendering and he came out of cover. He got to within three yards of the pill-box when the Spandau machine-gun erupted, spraying his body with bullets. Lassen reeled back and fell to the ground but as he fell, he threw three more hand-grenades, wiping out the Germans in the box.

Stephenson saw Lassen fall and raced to him. He was lying on his back, his body riddled with bullets, but he was still conscious. Stephenson cradled Lassen's limp body in his arms.

'I'm going to die,' Lassen said weakly. 'You must try and get the others out.'

Just then the redoubtable O'Reilly came forward and the two men tried to move Lassen but it was impossible. O'Reilly was already seriously wounded. Stephenson gave Lassen a shot of morphine but he knew it was only a hopeless gesture. Lassen was beyond help.

'It's no use,' Lassen gasped. 'I'm dying. Leave me and get away with the others.'

Lassen fought against death but it was the one battle he had to lose. He died where he lay. Less than a month later, the Second World War ended and Lassen's Denmark was liberated.

Anders Lassen had never faltered in consistently displaying supreme courage throughout his war. In that last action it was clear that, but for his single-handed attack, the entire patrol would have been massacred. For this, he was posthumously awarded the Victoria Cross, Britain's highest award for valour. Only twice before had it been awarded to foreigners – and they were both Danes.

Bibliography

In the course of research, the author has referred to some of the books listed below for technical and background information. They are highly recommended.

Appleyard, J. E., *Geoffrey* (Blandford Press, 1946)

Burrows, William E., *Richthofen* (Hart-Davis, 1970)

Farago, Ladislas, *The Game of the Foxes* (Hodder & Stoughton, 1972)

Hardwick, Michael, *The World's Greatest Air Mysteries* (Odhams, 1970)

Hart, Sir Basil Liddell, *History of the First World War* (Cassell, 1970)

Lassen, Suzanne, *Anders Lassen VC* (Muller, 1965)

Masterman, J. C., *The Double-Cross System* (Yale University Press, 1972)

Newman, Bernard, *Spy and Counter-Spy* (Robert Hale, 1970)

—— *The World of Espionage* (Souvenir Press, 1962)

Norris, Geoffrey, *The Royal Flying Corps* (Muller, 1965)

Oughton, Frederick, *Mannock VC* (Neville Spearman, 1958)

Pluschow, Gunther, *My Escape from Donington Hall* (Bodley Head)

Pudney, John, *Six Great Aviators* (Hamish Hamilton, 1955)

Rawlings, John, *Fighter Squadrons of the RAF* (Macdonald, 1969)

Rue, Jacques De La, *The History of the Gestapo* (Macdonald, 1964)

Saundby, Sir Robert, *Early Aviation* (Macdonald, 1971)

Saunders, Hilary St George, *The Green Beret* (Michael Joseph, 1949)

Whiting, Charles, *The Battle for Twelveland* (Leo Cooper, 1975)

Wighton, Charles, *The World's Greatest Spies* (Odhams, 1962)

Williams, Eric, *More Escapers* (Collins, 1968)